GW00891814

South Africa

Ian Phillips

Holmes McDougall, Edinburgh

Acknowledgements

The author and the publisher acknowledge the following illustration sources. They have made every effort to trace the copyright holders but where they have failed, they will be happy to make the necessary arrangements at the first opportunity.

We are grateful to the following for permission to reproduce illustrations:

Anti-Apartheid Movement   **117** (top)
Associated Press   **79**
BBC Hulton Picture Library   **14, 15, 19, 21, 51**
Camera Press   **31, 52, 103**
Cape Times   **99** (bottom)
Mary Evans   **12**
Les Gibbard   **97** (top)
International Defence and Aid Fund   **12, 20, 35, 36** (top), **39, 41, 42, 44** (top and bottom), **48, 49, 50, 54, 55, 56** (top and bottom), **57** (top), **60, 63, 64, 67, 69, 70, 72, 73, 74, 75** (top and bottom), **76** (top and bottom), **82, 85, 86, 87, 89, 90** (top and bottom), **93** (bottom), **94, 95, 97** (bottom), **98, 101, 102, 105, 107, 113**
International Freedom Foundation   **117** (bottom)
Popperfoto   **13, 18, 36** (bottom), **93** (top), **99** (top)
Rand Daily Mail   **83**
South African Museum   **9**

The author and publisher wish to thank the following who have given permission for the use of copyright material:

BBC Books for extracts from *The White Tribe of Africa* by David Harrison, 1981; Jonathan Cape Ltd. for extracts from *The Washing of the Spears* by Donald Morris, 1966; Frank Cass & Co. Ltd. for an extract from *The History of the Battles and Adventures of the British, Boers and Zulu in South Africa* by Duncan Campbell Francis Moodie, 1968; Wm. Collins & Co. Ltd. for extracts from *Naught for Your Comfort* by Trevor Huddleston, 1956, and *Let My People Go* by Albert Luthuli, 1962; *The Guardian* for numerous extracts; Hodder & Stoughton Ltd. for an extract from *Black and Gold* by Anthony Sampson, 1987; International Broadcasting Trust for an extract from *Spear of the Nation*, 1986; International Defence and Aid Fund for Southern African Publications for extracts from *The South African Reich* by Brian Bunting, 1987, *Struggle for a Birthright* by Mary Benson, 1985, *The Struggle is My Life* by Nelson Mandela, 1986, *Window on Soweto* by Joyce Sikakane, 1976, and *Brutal Force* by Gavin Cawthra, 1986; Methuen & Co. Ltd. for extracts from *South Africa* by Graham Leach, 1987; Mitchell Beazley Ltd. for an extract from *The Story of Africa* by Basil Davidson, 1984; *The Observer* for an extract which was published on 27th September 1987; Penguin Books Ltd. for extracts from *Biko* by Donald Woods, 1978, *The African Past* edited by Basil Davidson, 1966, *Path of Blood* by Peter Becker, 1979, *Cape to Cairo* by Mark Strange, 1973, *The Kaiser and His Times* by Michael Balfour, 1975, *To the Bitter End* by Emanoel Lee, 1986, *The Apartheid Handbook* by Roger Omond, 1986, *Mission To South Africa* by the Commonwealth Eminent Persons Group, 1986, *Part of My Soul* by Winnie Mandela, 1985, *Nelson Mandela* by Mary Benson, 1986, *The Sanctions Handbook* by Roger Omond and Joseph Hanlon, 1987, *Apartheid in Crisis* edited by M. Uhlig, 1986, *Apartheid's Second Front* by Joseph Hanlon, 1986, *Asking For Trouble* by Donald Woods, 1980; The South African Bureau of Information for extracts from *Talking With the ANC* produced in 1986, and the *Southern Africa Facts Sheet*, April and June 1986; *The Times* for extracts which appeared on 22nd March 1960; Unwin Hyman for an extract from *Southern Africa* by Parker & Pfukani, 1984; United Nations Publications for extracts from *Apartheid in Practice*, 1976.

For Jamie, Ben and Sam

Illustrations by Denby Design

Cover pictures by permission of the International Defence and Aid Fund (bottom photograph by Ingrid Gavshon)

Holmes McDougall Ltd, Allander House, 137-141 Leith Walk, Edinburgh EH6 8NS

ISBN 0 7157 2771 0

Printed and bound in Great Britain by Holmes McDougall, Edinburgh

Contents

South Africa Today

In 1985 and 1986 South Africa was the major international news story. Reports on television and in the press showed scenes of violence and unrest in the black townships. Since the elections in May 1987 the picture is more confusing. Reports from South Africa are less frequent and the situation has become even harder to follow. It is difficult to know exactly what is happening, as the headlines in Source 1 show:

SOURCE 1 — Newspaper Headlines May 1987-March 1988
SOUTH AFRICA'S RIGHT-TURN ALARMS BLACK LEADERS.
AIRPORT VIOLENCE GREETS RETURNING SOUTH AFRICAN WHITES.
PRETORIA CLAMPS DOWN ON PRESS FREEDOM.
ANC GUERILLAS KILLED IN BORDER CLASH.
APARTHEID'S CHILDREN.
ANC LEADER IS FREED FROM PRISON.
ANGOLA SAYS SOUTH AFRICA BOMBED ARMY BASES.
BLACK CIVIL WAR IN NATAL.
PRETORIA BANS UDF IN NEW CRACKDOWN.
GOVERNMENT DEFEATED BY CONSERVATIVES IN BY-ELECTION.

◀ Just by looking at the headlines is it possible to say which show
1. that apartheid may be changing?
2. that the government is still repressive?
3. that there is a disagreement between white South Africans?
4. that there is a dispute between different black groups?

One of the headlines explains why it is difficult to find out easily what is happening today in South Africa. Other headlines show that apartheid may be changing, while others reveal that the government is unwilling to change its racial policies. It is also assumed that in South Africa the problem is simply one of black against white. The headlines reveal that there are serious disagreements between different black groups and between whites in South Africa.

If some of the stories behind the headlines are looked at in a little more detail they will show that the problems facing South Africa are not so straightforward.

SOURCE 2 — SOUTH AFRICA'S RIGHT-TURN ALARMS BLACK LEADERS
South Africa's black leaders reacted with shock to the outcome of the whites-only election, which saw major gains by right-wing extremists, as well as the return of the National Party with an improved majority.

Archbishop Desmond Tutu said the result heralded the 'darkest stage' in South Africa's history. The UDF the country's largest anti-apartheid grouping said the stage had been set 'for the deepening of the conflict'. Dr Allan Boesak said 'The government has made peaceful change impossible.'
(The Guardian, 8 May 1987.)

SOURCE 3 — EXTREMES IN SOUTH AFRICA'S WHITE ELECTION

The significance of the election is simple. For the first time since 1948 South Africa has an opposition in parliament which stands to the right of the government. Before the election the Progressive Federal Party was the main opposition. Its liberal policies made it the conscience of white South Africa. The PFP is no longer the opposition following Wednesday's thrashing.
(The Guardian, 8 May 1987.)

SOURCE 4 — AIRPORT VIOLENCE GREETS RETURNING SOUTH AFRICAN WHITES

Members of the AWB (Afrikaner Resistance Movement) were gunning for another 'traitor', Dr Frederik Slabbert. About 150 fascists turned out at Jan Smuts airport to try and give a rough welcome to Dr Slabbert and his party of whites returning from their journey to West Africa where they had discussed peace with the outlawed African National Congress. 'We're waiting for Slabbert to smash his head in,' shouted one of the reception party.
(The Guardian, 22 July 1987.)

SOURCE 5 — PRETORIA CLAMPS DOWN ON PRESS FREEDOM

The Government has announced new emergency measures against South African papers. The new regulations will enable a minister to suspend publications which promote 'unlawful organisations' or stir up 'feelings' against the army or police.
(The Guardian, 28 August 1987.)

SOURCE 6 — ANC GUERILLAS KILLED IN BORDER CLASH

Three African National Congress guerillas were killed near the border with Zimbabwe in a two-day running battle with security forces. Three AK 47 rifles, eight pistols and a number of grenades were seized by soldiers.
(The Guardian, 14 September 1987.)

SOURCE 7 — ANC LEADER IS FREED FROM PRISON

Govan Mbeki, the former chairman of the outlawed African National Congress was last night released after more than 23 years in prison. His release will lead to speculation that the two other major ANC figures in prison, Nelson Mandela and Walter Sisulu may be released in the coming months.
(The Guardian, 6 November 1987.)

SOURCE 8 — APARTHEID'S CHILDREN

Sixteen-year-old Buras Nhlabathi was detained by South African police officers a year ago. Last week he told me part of his story: 'It was about 3.30 in the morning when they came to my house, then took me to the police station. There one of them hit me on the back. I fell down. They beat me for 45 minutes and I was then tortured for five hours.

They hit me with keys and pipes and sjamboks. I had no sleep. They kept me on my feet. Then they took me to the electric shock room where there were bright lights. They gave me shocks to my hands. Then they put me in the fridge room for 30 minutes. It was so cold I could not stop trembling.
(Glenys Kinnock writing in The Observer, 27 September 1987.)

Introduction

SOURCE 9 — ANGOLA SAYS SOUTH AFRICA BOMBED ARMY BASES

South African forces are bombing and shelling army positions in Southern Angola with the aim of capturing key towns and extending their military invasion further north the Angolan Defence Ministry said.
(The Guardian, 15 January 1988.)

SOURCE 10 — BLACK CIVIL WAR IN NATAL

A civil war between black and black is raging in South Africa. The conflict between the Zulu Inkatha movement and the UDF, the country's main anti-apartheid group, is continuing to escalate. With over 250 dead last year, the fighting has claimed more than 60 lives already this month.
(The Guardian, 25 January 1988.)

SOURCE 11 — PRETORIA BANS UDF IN NEW CRACKDOWN

The South African Government yesterday moved to silence all the leading voices of opposition by effectively banning 17 organisations and restricting the powerful Congress of South African Trade Unions to a purely trade union role. The crackdown stunned many people and drew warnings from anti-apartheid leaders that it would be interpreted — in the words of Archbishop Desmond Tutu — as a 'declaration of war'.

Its timing was widely seen as an attempt to win back white support for the National Party in advance of two by-elections next week.
(The Guardian, 25 February 1988.)

SOURCE 12 — GOVERNMENT DEFEATED BY CONSERVATIVES IN BY-ELECTION

President P. W. Botha yesterday implied that Archbishop Desmond Tutu and his civil rights marchers were to blame for the setback suffered by the ruling National Party at the hands of the extreme right wing Conservative Party in two by-elections.
(The Guardian, 4 March 1988.)

◀ After reading carefully through the sources what questions would you need to ask to understand more fully the background to the situation today in South Africa?

◀ Using your answers for the first question, which was based only on the headlines, can you use the twelve sources to justify your answers?

These brief items of news may help us to understand what has been happening in South Africa recently, but if you have tried to answer the second question you will appreciate that to get behind the news stories you require a great deal more information. As with so many modern-day issues, the roots of the problem are to be found in the past.

Apartheid is the one word which is associated with South Africa. Literally it means *apartness*. The policy of apartheid may be the cause of South Africa's problems, but policies are made by politicians, by people. To understand apartheid we need to ask several questions:
Who are the Afrikaners?
How did the policy of apartheid develop?
Why do the Afrikaners support apartheid?
Do English-speaking South Africans support apartheid?
How have the Africans reacted to apartheid?
Why should South Africa be isolated in the world?

If you are able to answer some of these questions you might come closer to understanding the problems facing South Africa today.

Finally, if you should doubt the importance of history in modern-day South Africa, look at the importance of 1988 for the Afrikaner:

500th anniversary of the 'discovery' of South Africa.

300th anniversary of the arrival of the first French Huguenots.

150th anniversary of the Great Trek.

80th anniversary of the National Convention which led to the formation of the Union of South Africa.

40th anniversary of the election of the National party and the policy of apartheid.

30th anniversary of Hendrik Verwoerd becoming Prime Minister.

10th anniversary of P. W. Botha becoming leader of South Africa.

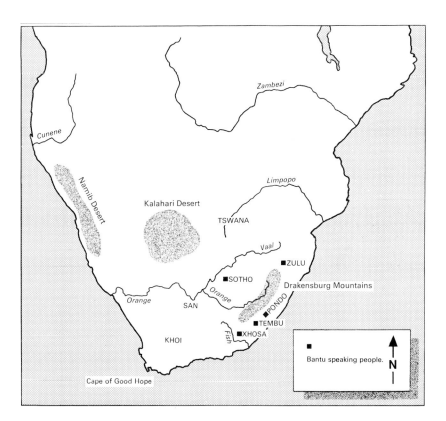

South Africa — physical features and patterns of settlement. This shows distribution of tribal groups at the time of early Dutch settlement in the 17th century. As can be seen, Bantu-speaking groups were established in areas of South Africa.

Chapter 1

The Settlement of South Africa

This chapter deals with the following topics:

1. The European settlement of South Africa.
2. The Afrikaner version of settlement in South Africa.
3. The archaeological and oral evidence surrounding the settlement of South Africa.

After reading this chapter and completing the exercises you will have:
1. Looked at conflicting opinions surrounding the settlement and colonisation of South Africa.
2. Discovered why the Afrikaners place so much importance on this early period of colonisation.

The European settlement of South Africa is surrounded by controversy. While the Portuguese were the first Europeans to land at the Cape of Good Hope in 1488, it was the Dutch who established the first permanent settlement in the mid-17th century.

Today the Afrikaners, descendants of the Dutch colonists, claim that South Africa was then an empty land and therefore they have an equal claim to the territory with the Africans. This is still the view of the settlement of South Africa and one which is still taught in South African schools. This may be the official view, but is it true? It seems that the events of 300 years ago still have an importance in the late 20th century.

◄ Using the map on page 7, describe the main physical features of South Africa and the areas of tribal settlement.

European Settlers: Interpreting the Evidence

An important part of Afrikaner history taught in all South African schools is that the Bantu and the Europeans began to settle in what is now South Africa at the same time.

SOURCE 13 — The Bantu migration

Until the 16th century the Bushmen remained in undisputed possession of their land. Then many other people migrated to South Africa from the north and the south.

During the 17th century, while the Europeans explored the Cape, there was a great migration of dark-skinned Africans southward from the vicinity of the equator. The people now called the Bantu reached South Africa at approximately the same time that Europeans began to move north.

(A South African school history textbook.)

Pottery figure found in the Transvaal dating from 500 AD. Further evidence of settlement of South Africa many years before the arrival of Europeans.

SOURCE 14 — The white settlement of South Africa

It is nonsense to suppose that the interior of Southern Africa belonged to the Bantu and that the white man took it away from him. The Bantus penetrated from the north almost at the same time as the white man entered the south. They had equal title to the country. The Voortrekkers wished to partition the country and live in peace, because they had already experienced enough trouble in the Cape. But the Bantu were not amenable to reason. They respected only one thing, and that was force.
(The Official Guide Book to the Voortrekker Memorial.)

SOURCE 15 — A black South African's view of white settlement

No part of South Africa can be regarded as exclusively white, nor can we accept the fact that there were large parts of our country which were empty. Our people were pastoralists who moved their herds from place to place; who ploughed land and who allowed it to lie fallow if it became worked out. You cannot say to a man that this land is not yours because I did not find you at this particular place at this particular time. South Africa is a very big country; when the whites arrived in 1652 there were perhaps 2 million black South Africans. You could not have occupied every inch of South Africa but this country is ours.
(Nthatho Motlana, speaking on Granada Television's series 'Apartheid'.)

SOURCE 16 — A modern day historian comments on the South African view of history

According to a white South African myth, the Bantu crossed the Limpopo from the North into what is now the Transvaal at just the same time as the Dutchmen were stepping ashore at the Cape.

This myth is held in high regard by white South Africans, but is historically absurd. The ancestors of the Bantu language peoples of modern South Africa, Zulu, Xhosa and many others, had certainly established themselves by AD 400 in the territory that was to be named the Transvaal 14 centuries later.
(Basil Davidson, 'The Story of Africa', Mitchell Beazley, 1984.)

SOURCE 17 — A white South African comments on the official view of settlement

School-children in South Africa are taught that the arrival of the white settlers coincided with the arrival of Bantu tribesmen, but radio-carbon dating provides evidence of Negroid communities in the Transvaal as early as the fifth century AD. The southward migration of the Bantu speakers to the shores of the country was considerable in the fourteenth century and they were certainly established as far as the Gamtoos River in the Cape Province by the fifteenth century.
('Biko', Donald Woods, Penguin Books, 1978.)

Questions
1. Using all the sources, can you sum up the two conflicting views of the settlement of South Africa?
2. How might a white South African use parts of Source 15 to argue his 'equal claim' to an empty land?
3. In what ways might the archaeological evidence be said to be neutral? Do you think this makes it more important as a source of evidence?
4. Is Basil Davidson in agreement with the Afrikaner view? Does he give any clues as to why the Afrikaner has this view of the settlement of South Africa?
5. Do you think that these arguments over the settlement of South Africa are relevant to the present day?

The People of South Africa

This chapter deals with the ideas, beliefs and way of life of the following:

1. the Afrikaners.
2. the native Africans.

When you have read this chapter and completed the exercises you will have:

1. Understood the factors which shape the attitudes of the Afrikaner.
2. Looked at the traditional way of life of the black people of South Africa and their early conflicts with the white settlers.

Most of the present difficulties facing South Africa arise out of the conflicting attitudes and opinions of the many different racial groups. It is much more complex than a simple dispute between recently-arrived European settlers and the native Africans.

The descendants of the first European settlers, the Dutch, regard themselves as white Africans. Some say this is what the word *Afrikaner* means; they have also been described as the 'White Tribe of Africa'.

With a history of 300 years behind them they have not only developed their own language — Afrikaans — but their own culture and way of life. While one cannot say that all Afrikaners have the same ideas and values, it is possible to make some general observations about their outlook. Many are very religious and the Dutch Reformed Church has played a significant role in developing social as well as political ideas. Family ties are also of considerable importance. What is more, Afrikaners are fiercely independent, valuing their own freedom and resenting outside interference.

Afrikaners are also patriotic and very proud of their past. Their outlook on life has been conditioned by the hardships and struggles involved in building a nation in a new land. There are many similarities between the Afrikaner and the frontiersman of the American west. The common hardships and their history of struggle — against the land, the native people and the British — have given the Afrikaners a sense of identity. They refer to themselves as the Volk — the people, but it can also mean the community.

SOURCE 18 — Afrikaner religion

God created us differently and it is to the honour of God that we must preserve that difference. God gave mankind Ten Commandments and one of them said, 'Honour thy father and thy mother.' That means it is not just a matter of being obedient to your parents. You must also honour your parents and preserve their identity.

(Koot Vorster, Elder in the Dutch Reformed Church. 'The White Tribe of Africa', David Harrison, BBC Publications, 1981.)

◀ Sources 18 and 19 provide you with information about the Afrikaner's religious ideas. How could you use these sources to justify these statements?
a. The Afrikaners were very religious.
b. Their ideas about the native African people were influenced by their understanding of the Old Testament.

SOURCE 19 — The Afrikaner and the Bible

The Afrikaners believed that the Africans were the children of Ham — one of Noah's sons in the Bible. Ham displeased God and he and his descendants — the people of Canaan — were condemned to be the servants of Noah's other children. To the Afrikaner, being a servant and a slave were the same thing. It was, therefore, written in the Bible that the Africans were to be the slaves of the White Europeans.

◀ The Battle of Blood River took place in 1838 and every year Afrikaners remember the battle and the promise that you can read in Source 20. Does this source provide any evidence to show how important the past is to the Afrikaner? How might Source 21 be able to help you answer this question?

SOURCE 20 — The Afrikaner Oath at the Battle of Blood River Memorial

Here we stand before the Holy God of Heaven and earth, to make him a vow that if he will protect us and deliver the enemy into our hands we will observe this day each year as a day of thanksgiving, like a sabbath. And we will also make our children take part with us for all the coming generations.

SOURCE 21 — Afrikaner attitudes to the British

The only conclusion I could draw from the war (against the British) is that Milner and Kitchener (the British leaders) were out to break the backbone of the Afrikaner, and their backbone consisted of their womenfolk. And to destroy as many women and children as they could. It wasn't war it was deliberate murder.

When we made peace in 1902 it was an understanding between the leaders of the Afrikaner people that they would fight for their freedom at the very first opportunity.

(Henning Klopper, an Afrikaner politician, from 'The White Tribe of Africa', David Harrison, BBC Publications, 1981.)

SOURCE 22 — Afrikaners and Africans

Apartheid can be described as a policy of good neighbourliness. If gradual separation develops and each group gets his full opportunities with his own people then he can go anywhere. While the white man will remain the ruler of South Africa he, as the guardian of the black man, will see to it that his development does take place.

(Hendrik Verwoerd's description of apartheid.)

◀ Sources 22 and 23 describe the Afrikaner's attitude to the Africans in the 20th century. Are there any differences between the sources in their attitude to the non-European population of South Africa?

SOURCE 23 — The Africans and the Constitution

In obedience to God Almighty and His Holy Word. Every coloured group of races will be segregated not only as regards the place of dwelling but also with regard to the place of work.

(Extract from the National Party Draft Constitution drawn up during the Second World War. 'The South African Reich', Brian Bunting, IDAF Publications, reprinted 1987.)

The Native Africans

The present government in South Africa does not recognise the native black Africans as one people. It points out that in the past the Africans belonged to one of several tribes or nations. However, such tribal divisions have become less important as South Africa has become an industrialised and urban nation. The government has never suggested that the European population should be similarly divided into Afrikaner and English groups.

The tribal divisions are based on language and way of life. The two main language groups are the Khoisan and the Bantu. The Khoisan are thought to be the original inhabitants of Southern Africa. One group of Khoisan are the 'bushmen', a name given them by the first Dutch settlers. The bushmen were nomadic hunters living in small family groups. They had no permanent villages and did not grow crops or keep animals.

Another tribe of the Khoisan group were the Hottentot, a name given to them by the Dutch, though they called themselves the Khoikhoi. They were in the area of the Cape and followed a more settled existence living in villages herding sheep and cattle. Close contact with the Dutch settlers was disastrous for the Khoikhoi. Their independent way of life was destroyed by epidemics of smallpox in the 18th century. Many became slaves working for the Europeans, others intermarried and many of their descendants today make up the Coloured population, most of whom live in the Cape.

The largest number of blacks in South Africa today belong to the group of Bantu-speaking Africans. They originally came from Central Africa and gradually moved south. The Bantu in Southern Africa were traditionally farmers, herding cattle and growing cereal crops like millet. They were well organised into tribes and knew how to work metal for tools and weapons.

Within this main group of Bantu there were two important divisions: the Sotho and the Nguni — again a division based on language. Two of the largest tribes or nations in South Africa, the Zulu and the Xhosa, belong to the Nguni group of Bantu languages. Due to their more settled way of life, the Nguni and the Sotho offered more resistance to the Europeans as they moved north and east. The 19th century was marked by a series of clashes between Europeans and Africans and the issue was always land. In the face of modern weapons it was the Africans who had to give up their land.

Khoisan village in the Cape. The Khoisan were nomadic herders who drove their animals to new pastures when the grazing was exhausted. Their villages were temporary and the huts could be dismantled and carried with them.

SOURCE 24 — The Khoisan
The Hottentots who live in these parts seldom make use of any weapons. Here and there a man will furnish himself with a spear called a *hassegai**, by way of defence against wolves.

Their houses are as simple as their dress and adapted to the wandering pastoral life they lead. Their dwellings scarcely merit any other name than that of huts. They are sufficient for the

Hottentot's wants and desires. He may, therefore, be considered a happy man. In their *Kraal* or village, the huts are all built exactly alike.

* This is also known as an assegai.

('A Voyage to the Cape of Good Hope 1772 – 1776', by Andrew Sparrman in 'The African Past', edited by Basil Davidson, Penguin Books, 1966.)

SOURCE 25 — The Zulu way of life

Zululand was a land of plenty; at regular intervals beehive huts straddled mountain slopes perched on the banks of streams. There was an abundance of game and skilful hunters seldom failed to keep cooking pots replenished with meat.

In the fields beside the huts the women sang in chorus as they cleared the crops of weeds. In the cattlefold cows were milked by herd boys and the oxen inspected by the men for disease and injury. The status of the chiefs was determined by the number of cattle they owned. Cattle were only slaughtered for ritual purposes; beef was a delicacy eaten only when a beast had died. Cattle provided the settlements with milk, butter, hides for clothing and dung for plastering hut floors and for lining and sealing grain pits.

('Path of Blood' by Peter Becker, Penguin Books, 1979.)

SOURCE 26 — Cetswayo and the British

Some years ago the Natal Land and Colonial Company made a proposal to me to try and secure for them the title of a certain tract of land in Zulu country. Accordingly I spoke to Cetswayo on the subject:

'Yes, what you say is very good, but our land is our home, we don't like parting with it, besides we are afraid of you white men. If we give you a piece of land for more than one to live on, they will want more, and so on until they get the whole and we will have to wander about as if we had no land.'

('The History of the Battles and Adventures of the British, Boers and Zulu in South Africa' by Duncan Campbell Francis Moodie, Frank Cass & Co. Ltd., 1968.)

A Zulu village. The Zulu belonged to the Nguni and lived a more settled existence. They had their own tribal lands. Crops were an important part of their livelihood. When soil lost its fertility it was left fallow and new land was cultivated.

SOURCE 27 — The start of the Zulu war

After pressure from Boers living close to Zululand and a series of border incidents, British colonial officials in Natal met with Zulu leaders and issued a series of demands. Cetswayo had 20 days to comply with the demands or face the consequences.

The Zulu inDuna (council) were unable to grasp the significance of the demands. They pointed out that the rivers were in flood and the cattle could not be collected in 20 days and they took exception to a message which implied that Cetswayo was a cruel and oppressive tyrant. 'Have Zulus complained?' growled one of them. The inDuna were fearful of reporting to Cetswayo and it was two weeks before they reached Ulundi (the Zulu capital).
('The Washing of the Spears', Donald Morris, Jonathan Cape, 1966.)

SOURCE 28 — The Battle of Isandhlwana

The Zulus departed Isandhlwana. The spears had been washed. There had been almost 1800 men in the camp at noon. By late evening 55 Europeans were still alive. The Zulus had given battle with a high hearted courage that bullets had not been able to stop and their losses had been fearful.

'An assegai has been thrust into the belly of the nation, there are not enough tears to mourn for the dead', Cetswayo said when the news reached him. There was never a count, but over 2000 Zulus were dead, and scores dragged themselves away to die for miles about the camp.
('The Washing of the Spears', Donald Morris, Jonathan Cape, 1966.)

The Battle of Isandhlwana. The army of Cetswayo wiped out an entire column when the British army invaded Zulu land. Their success threatened the colony of Natal.

Questions

1. What were the main differences in the way of life of:
   a. the Khoisan and
   b. the Nguni?
2. How far do the sources help you to understand why the Nguni and the Sotho put up a greater resistance to European settlers in the 19th century?
3. From Sources 26 and 27 do you think Cetswayo was right to be suspicious of the British in Natal?
4. At the Battle of Isandhlwana the Zulu forces inflicted a serious defeat on the British, but what do you think Cetswayo meant when he said that an 'assegai had been thrust into the belly of the nation'?

The Great Trek

This chapter deals with the following topics:
1. The conflict between the Boers and the British authorities
2. The events of the Great Trek
3. The dangers facing the Trekkers.

After you have read this chapter and completed the exercises you will have:
1. Looked at the long-term causes of the disagreement between the Boers and the British.
2. Examined the motives of the Trekkers.
3. Examined the events which led to the Trek.
4. Looked at the importance of the Trek for modern-day Afrikaners.

After 1820 British settlers began to arrive in the Cape in growing numbers. The Boers saw their independent way of life being threatened. English became the language of government, Dutch officials were replaced by British magistrates. British laws treated black and white equally. The Boers began to feel like outsiders in their own land.

The Boer farmstead shows the isolated and simple way of life that many Boers lived. Most were subsistence farmers employing Africans as labourers.

There were important religious differences between the Boers and the British. Boer religion taught that the African was inferior and the Bible condemned the African to a life of slavery. British missionaries in the Cape were trying to convert Africans to Christianity. The Boers, too, found this unacceptable and against their religious ideas. By the 1830s the Boers began to consider moving away from the Cape, away from British control, free to live 'beyond the sight of one's neighbour's smoke'. The Trekkers saw themselves as the children of Israel, fleeing from Egypt to the promised land.

Anna Steenkamp, one of the Trekkers, explains the reasons for leaving the Cape.

SOURCE 29 — Leaving the Cape

It was not so much the freeing of the slaves that drove us to leave as much as the Kaffir* being placed on an equal footing with Christians, contrary to the laws of God and the natural distinctions of race and religion, so that it was intolerable for any decent Christian to bow beneath such a yoke. We withdrew in order to preserve our doctrine* in purity.

* Kaffir: an insulting term for an African.
* Doctrine: a set of religious or political ideas.

Piet Retief, one of the leaders of the Trek, explains why the Boers left the Cape.

SOURCE 30 — Retief's Manifesto

We despair of saving the colony from the evils which threaten it.

We complain of severe losses which we have been forced to sustain by the emancipation* of our slaves.

We complain of the continual plunder which we have endured from the Kaffirs and by the last invasion of the colony which desolated the frontier districts.

We quit this colony under the full assurance that the English government will allow us to govern ourselves in the future.

* Emancipation: granting freedom to slaves.

Question
What complaints did the Boers have about British rule in the Cape?

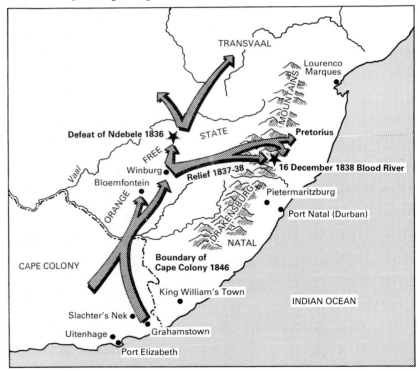

The Great Trek is seen as an heroic event in the history of the Afrikaner and contributed to their strong sense of independence.

The Great Trek: Motives of the Trekkers

Packing their few belongings into wagons, and driving their cattle with them, the Boers began to leave the Cape. There was not one 'Great Trek', but a series over a period of years. Altogether it is estimated that 14,000 people left the Cape between 1836 and 1839. They were setting off into the unknown. The Trekkers who made for Natal had to cross the Drakensberg Mountains, a formidable barrier for ox-wagons.

All the Trekkers faced the dangers of drought, disease and, above all, Africans who resented the white man coming to settle on their land.

Retief's group came into conflict with the Zulu. This struggle has become an important part of the history of the Trek. Piet Retief was killed on the orders of Dingaan, the Zulu chief, in an incident which portrays Dingaan as brutal and treacherous. The massacre of Retief's party was avenged by Andries Pretorius at the Battle of Blood River. There a small group of Boer commandos defeated a Zulu army of 10,000. The Boer state of Natalia was short-lived; the British took over the colony in 1843 and the Boers packed up their belongings and trekked back over the Drakensberg Mountains, finding independence in the Transvaal and the Orange Free State. The Trek passed into Afrikaner history and legend. In 1938, on a hilltop outside Pretoria, work on the Voortrekker Monument was begun. Its aim: to remind the Afrikaners of their ancestors who set up the first free Afrikaner republics.

A guide at the Voortrekker Monument describes the massacre of the Trekkers by Dingaan.

SOURCE 31 — Massacre

Dingaan was the Zulu King; to them he's a god. With a flick of his hand he can cause your death. When you come to him you kneel down. Retief had drawn up a written contract. Before witnesses Dingaan is actually making his cross on it. Because of course he can't read. But the signing of the Treaty meant nothing. At a word from Dingaan, Retief and his whole party were cruelly done to death. You see the clubs and the native holding a rock. They were all killed every one of them.

Dingaan was not satisfied; three Zulu regiments attacked the Boer families waiting in the foothills. The Zulu fell on the defenceless wagons in the blackness of night. Forty men, fifty women and one hundred and eighty children perished.

The same guide then describes how the Boers led by Andries Pretorius defeated the Zulu and avenged the massacre of Retief and his men.

SOURCE 32 — The Boers' revenge

As battle approached they vowed that if God gave them victory they would keep that day forever as a day of thanksgiving.

On the night of 15 December the commando was in position on the banks of the river, the oxen and horses were all inside the laager. At dawn the whole Zulu kingdom sat there. Ten thousand warriors at least. Six hours later three thousand Zulu lay dead, their assegais (spears) no match for guns. The river ran with their blood. The trekkers suffered three wounded. It was a brilliant victory, at what was known from that day as the Battle of Blood River. Now every year on 16 December, at hundreds of services all over South Africa, the Afrikaner gives thanks and renews the vow the trekkers took before the battle.

Afrikaners describe their involvement with the re-enactment of the Trek in 1938.

SOURCE 33 — The Trek re-enacted

For years I had dreamed of retracing the steps of the Voortrekkers in a pilgrimage across South Africa.

You have no idea what emotion it caused. I saw people in tears because of this intense wave of patriotism, of pride in this romantic page in our history. We never had a symbol before; the ox-wagon became that symbol.

The whole feeling of the trek was that it was the will and work of the Almighty God. It was a pilgrimage, a sacred happening.

We arrived on 16 December: there were a quarter of a million people there. An Afrikaner said to me 'Now we're going to knock the hell out of the English.' It was a lonely and terrible occasion for any English-speaking South African. One man was shouted down because he gave his greeting in English.

Basil Davidson, a modern-day historian, gives his assessment of the Great Trek.

SOURCE 34

Finding the liberalism of the Cape government both inconvenient and 'un-Christian', groups of Dutch-speaking settlers began moving North in a ragged migration known in their history rather pretentiously as the 'Great Trek'.

The Voortrekker Monument, Pretoria. The importance of the Trek for the Afrikaner is illustrated by this monument which was built to commemorate the centenary of the Trek. The re-enactment of the Trek in 1938 made an important contribution to the growing popularity of the National Party.

Questions

1. From Source 29, what were the religious differences between the Boers and the British which led to the Boers leaving the Cape?
2. From Source 30, did Piet Retief give any political or economic reasons for quitting the colony?
3. Sources 31 and 32 are a written version from a guided tour of the Voortrekker Monument. What do these sources, the map of the Great Trek on page 16 and the picture of the Voortrekker Monument above, tell you about the Afrikaners' attitude to their history? How does Source 33 help you to answer this question?
4. Explain what Basil Davidson's attitude towards the Great Trek is? Do you agree or disagree with his view?

The Boer War I

The following pages deal with the following topics:
1. The discovery of gold in the Transvaal
2. The Uitlanders
3. British interests in the Transvaal.

After reading these two pages and completing the following exercises you will have:
1. Examined the causes of the conflict between Britain and the Boer Republics.
2. Discovered that the causes can be divided into three
   i   economic
   ii social and
   iii political.

Following the Great Trek the Boers enjoyed a form of independence in the Orange Free State and the Transvaal. This was changed by the discovery of diamonds and gold towards the end of the 19th century. The potential wealth of the Transvaal was to threaten Boer independence, as thousands of miners flocked to the area.

Johannesburg grew from a mining encampment to the second biggest town in South Africa in just a few years. Most of the miners were British, but to the Boers they were all outsiders — Uitlanders.

The Boers despised the incomers' greed and their godless way of life. Above all, the Boers felt threatened, they saw that their way of life was in danger of being swamped. To ensure that their way of life continued the Transvaal government refused to allow the Uitlanders any political rights, while at the same time making them pay high taxes.

In 1895 Cecil Rhodes tried to use the complaints of the Uitlanders to end the independence of the Transvaal. Troops of the British South Africa Company led by Dr Leander Starr Jameson would march on Johannesburg and overthrow the Boers. The episode was a disaster. The Uitlanders in Johannesburg did not revolt and Jameson's men were quickly halted, defeated and imprisoned.

Cecil Rhodes, businessman and Imperialist, who believed that his mission in Africa was to acquire new colonies for Britain.

SOURCE 35 — The complaints of the Uitlanders
They (the mine owners) did not like the excessive taxation. They resented the system of concessions granted by Kruger. The mine owners cried that 'No sooner does a commodity become essential than someone tries to get a concession for its supply.' In order to make their complaints appear less self-serving the Chamber of Mines in 1894 collected some 13,000 signatures on a petition demanding the right to vote.

19

Chapter 4

In 1895 five leading citizens of Johannesburg (including two mine owners and Cecil Rhodes' brother) sent this 'cry for help':

The position in this State has been so critical that there will be a conflict between the Government and the Uitlander population. Thousands of unarmed men, women and children of our own race will be at the mercy of well armed Boers.
(Mark Strange, 'Cape to Cairo', Penguin Books, 1973, pp. 135 & 138.)

◀ In Chapter 1 you read something about the ideas and values of the Afrikaners. From the description of Johannesburg in Source 36 can you suggest any reasons why the Afrikaners of the Transvaal would dislike the Uitlanders?
◀ Source 35 places a great deal of importance on the ill-treatment of the Uitlanders. How does Source 36 disagree with this view?
◀ What reasons do you think there might have been for this disagreement?

SOURCE 36 — The Boers and the Uitlanders
Under Kruger's rule the corrupting effects of gold had been contained. The Transvaal of 1895 was the sort of place which God himself would have approved.

With one glaring exception — Johannesburg. Streets of gorgeous shops and music halls, a race-course, circus and zoo, 650 licensed bars, unnumbered brothels and a Stock Exchange. The Uitlanders, who outnumbered the Transvaalers in Johannesburg by more than seven to one, were naturally denied the vote. Their petition was brushed aside by Kruger. 'If we give them the vote,' he told the Volksraad (the Transvaal Parliament), 'we may as well give up the republic.'

As he (Kruger) fully expected, the population of Johannesburg hardly looked up from its main occupation — making money — to voice a protest.
(Mark Strange 'Cape to Cairo', pp. 135 – 136, Penguin Books, 1973.)

Diamond mines in Kimberley. The discovery of the wealth of the Boer states in the late 19th century threatened Afrikaner independence. The illustration is also evidence for the part played by Africans in the development of the economic wealth of South Africa.

The Boer War II: A Study in Causation

SOURCE 37 — Boer reaction to the Jameson Raid

Before the Jameson Raid my father used to write letters in English. It was the smart thing to do for middle-class Afrikaners. After the Jameson Raid he never allowed English to be spoken in the house again.

Boer soldiers. Their equipment and tactics proved to be more than a match for the regular troops of the British Army. Their appearance made it difficult for the British to tell who was a farmer and who was a soldier.

SOURCE 38 — The Kruger Telegram

From His Imperial Majesty Kaiser Wilhelm II
To The President of the Transvaal Paulus Kruger:
I would like to express my sincere congratulations that you and your peoples have succeeded, without the help of friendly powers, in restoring peace in the face of armed bands which have broken into your country as disturbers of the peace and have been able to preserve the independence of your country against attacks from outside.
('The Kaiser and His Times', Michael Balfour, Penguin Books, 1975.) Kaiser Wilhelm had also considered sending German naval troops into the Transvaal through Portuguese East Africa.

SOURCE 39 — British reaction to the Jameson Raid

Winston Churchill wrote:
'Sooner or later, in a righteous cause or a picked quarrel, for the sake of our Empire, for the sake of our honour, for the sake of the race, we must fight the Boers.'

SOURCE 40 — President Kruger's decision to fight

Her Majesty's subjects demanded my trousers, I gave them and my coat likewise. They now want my life; I cannot grant them that. I shall give everything, everything, everything for peace. But if they touch my independence, I shall resist.

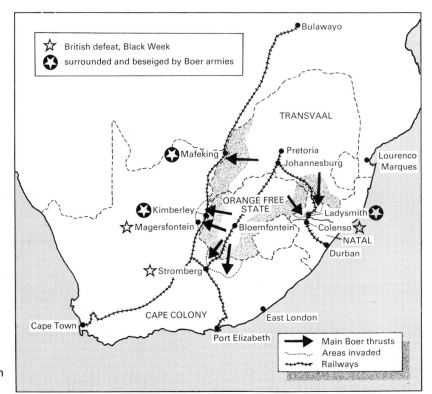

Black Week brought news of a series of unheard of disasters to the British Army in the opening stages of the Boer Wars.

Questions

1. How did the Afrikaners react to the Jameson Raid? Do you think that this might have been a typical Afrikaner attitude?

2. Using Source 40 and what you already know of the Afrikaner can you suggest any reasons for this reaction?

3. The Jameson Raid has been described as a humiliation for Britain; do you think that Winston Churchill's remark in Source 39 confirms this view?

4. Churchill also makes reference to the Empire. How do you think this comment might be related to Source 38?

5. Why do you think the Anglo-Boer War was fought?

The Boer War III

The next two pages deal with the following topics:
1. The tactics used by the Boers
2. How the British treated the Boers.

After you have read these pages and completed the exercises you will have:
1. Understood the Boer motives for fighting the war.
2. Discovered the consequences for future relations between Briton and Boer after the war.

By June 1900 a column of 50,000 men under Lord Roberts had advanced to Pretoria; en route most of the Boer towns had surrendered without a fight. It seemed that the war was almost over, but the Boer commandos had simply melted into the countryside. There began almost two years of guerilla war with no real front-line.

The greatest mistake the British Army made during the war was to think that the Boers would be no match for them. The Boer Army was certainly different. All men between the ages of 16 and 60 could serve in the army. Each man provided his own equipment. Boers 'going on commando' had to be ready at a moment's notice. They were organised in local or regional Commandos. It was a democratic army; orders and battle plans were debated by all regional commanders. The Boers were excellent marksmen and horsemen, they knew the land and they were fighting for their independence. It was to take a British army of 400,000 men two years before they finally defeated the Boer army of 60,000.

The Boers could live off the land, relying on their own people to feed and supply them. Under Lord Kitchener the British embarked on a controversial strategy. Boer families were driven off the land, their farms destroyed, crops burnt and animals killed. Boer women and children were herded into camps of concentration.

The destruction of Boer farms, burning crops and driving off animals marked a new phase in the war. It denied the Boers supplies and helped to end the war. The brutality of the policy caused long-term resentment.

SOURCE 41 — Boer fighting methods
The Boers fought as a team, not waiting for an order to take advantage of an opportunity or to retreat when threatened. Commandants preferred ambush to other methods of attack. They liked to fight on ground which had been carefully studied and marked for distance. To lie in wait on a suitable koppie (hillside) where they could hide behind large stones. When the shooting started their smokeless powder did not give away their location. If their position was threatened they would run and would soon be out of range.
(Emanoel Lee 'To the Bitter End', Penguin Books, 1986, p. 43.)

SOURCE 42 — The New British Policy
The General Commander in Chief is desirous that all possible means shall be taken to stop the present guerrilla warfare. One measure which has successfully been tried is the removal of all men, women and children, and natives from the Districts which the enemies' bands occupy. *(contd.)*

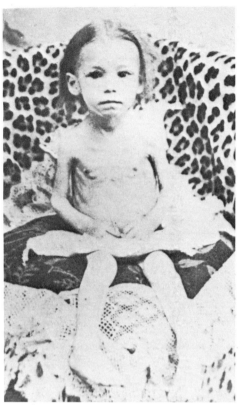

Boer families who were driven off farms were herded together in concentration camps. Overcrowding in huts and tents, inadequate water supplies and poor food lowered the inmates' resistance to disease which killed between 20,000 and 30,000. Most of the victims were women and children. The estimated Boer population in the Transvaal and the Orange Free State was around 100,000 before the war began.

The women and children brought in should be camped near the railway for supplies and should be divided into two categories: 1st Refugees and the families of neutrals. 2nd Those whose husbands, fathers and sons are on commando. The preference in accommodation, etc should be given to those in the first class.
(Memorandum from Lord Kitchener, Pretoria, 21 December 1900.)

SOURCE 43 — Conditions in the Camps of Concentration

Here some twenty to twenty-five persons were carried away daily — it was a death rate such as had never been known except in times of the Great Plague. The whole talk was of death — who died yesterday, who lay dying today and who would be dead tomorrow. After a while the corpses were carried away at dawn and instead of passing through the town approached the cemetery another way; many were buried in one grave. One small girl had lost six brothers and sisters in the Kroonstad Camp.
(Emily Hobhouse, 'The Brunt of War and Where it Fell'. Notes on the treatment of civilians in South Africa.)

SOURCE 44 — A British politician criticises Kitchener's tactics

Is this the way to make loyal British subjects of these people? Brave men will forget injustices to themselves more readily than they will insults and wrongs to their women and children. When children are being treated in this way and dying, we are simply ranging the deepest passions of the human heart against British rule in Africa. It will always be remembered that this is the way British rule started here, and this is the method by which it was brought about.
(Lloyd George speaking in the House of Commons, June 1901.)

Kitchener's tactics, however brutal, succeeded in wearing down the will of the Boers to fight. In May 1902 the Boer Generals reluctantly agreed to surrender. The Peace Treaty of Vereeniging brought the war to a close. The Boers agreed to recognise King Edward VII as their ruler. In return the British government promised to pay reparations for the damage to Boer property and to draw up a new constitution which promised a degree of independence for the Boers.

The British government was anxious to heal the wounds between the two sides. For some Boers the wounds were not so easily healed. The Anglo-Boer War was to be an important turning-point in relations between the Afrikaners and the English-speaking South Africans. The way the British had fought the war was to cause long-term resentment, which was an important factor in the rise of Afrikaner nationalism.

Questions

1. The British expected a quick victory against the Boers. Why do you think the British were so optimistic? How might Source 41 help you to answer this question?
2. How would Kitchener have justified the new British policy outlined in Source 42?
3. Using Source 43 and the pictures on page 23 and above can you describe the results of Kitchener's policy?
4. Do you think that the British public would have approved of Kitchener's methods?
5. Lloyd George in Source 44 spoke of the dangers of British policy. Using Henning Klopper's statement in Chapter 1 do you think that Lloyd George's opinions were correct?

The Rise of Afrikaner Nationalism

This chapter deals with the following topics:
1. The growth of Afrikaner Nationalism and the National Party
2. The problem of the Poor Whites
3. The development of racial laws.

After reading this chapter and completing the exercises you will have:
1. Understood the meaning of nationalism
2. Discovered the social and economic causes of Afrikaner Nationalism.
3. Seen that the creation of the National Party was a turning point in South African history.

In the new Union of South Africa, Jan Smuts and Louis Botha, both former Boer Generals, wanted to unite Boer and Briton. This was not popular with all Afrikaners, who felt that the British in South Africa were too powerful and that the British influence was too strong. Something had to be done to protect the traditional way of life of the Afrikaner, which was under threat; in schools his language was ridiculed and children were punished for speaking Afrikaans. Barry Hertzog, yet another Boer General, formed the Afrikaner National Party to look after the interests of the Afrikaners. When the First World War broke out many Afrikaners thought it was wrong for South Africa to fight against Germany who had earlier supported the Boers.

The combined effects of the Boer War, drought and economic depression following the First World War created hardship for many Boers. Many farmers faced ruin: driven off their land by the British and later ruined by drought. In search of work they flocked to the cities, where they lived in poverty. They had few skills and little education. Those who found work in the mines were poorly paid. English-speaking supervisors often told the Afrikaners that they preferred working with black miners.

After the First World War, urban whites faced desperate problems. Mine owners, in an attempt to reduce costs, tried to replace white workers with cheaper native labour. This provoked a bitter strike. Troops were called in and 39 miners were killed and four of the strike leaders were hanged for treason. Smuts was regarded as a traitor to the Afrikaner people for supporting the mine owners. In the 1924 elections Hertzog's National Party won. After 1924 the majority of Afrikaners voted for one of the Nationalist parties which promised to put their interests first.

SOURCE 45 — The problem of the Poor Whites
During a single day I came across half a dozen homes west of Pretoria where the descendants of those early settlers are today eking out a miserable existence by going into a native location and working for the more prosperous natives during the ploughing season.
(From an official report on the conditions of the poor whites. D Harrison, 'The White Tribe of Africa', BBC Publications, 1981, p. 73.)

SOURCE 46 — Afrikaner reaction to the Poor Whites
I have observed instances in which the children of Afrikaner families were running around as naked as kaffirs in Congoland. We have knowledge today of Afrikaner girls, so poor they work for coolies (Indians) and Chinese. They are all our flesh and blood; they carry our names; they are Afrikaners all of them, the children of Afrikaner martyrs.
(Part of a speech by D. W. Malan at a meeting discussing the problem of the poor whites. From D. Harrison, 'The White Tribe of Africa', BBC Publications, 1981, p. 71.)

◀ Why were so many whites living in poverty during the 1920s and 1930s?

Afrikaner Nationalism: A Turning Point in South Africa

SOURCE 47 — The treatment of Poor Whites
One of the senior officers on the railway said to me one day: Why do you want to come and work in a community like this? I'll see you get the sack, you Dutch bastard. That was common language here. They told me to my face that they preferred blacks to Afrikaners.
(Harrison, 'The White Tribe of Africa', p. 65.)

SOURCE 48 — Solving the problem of the Poor Whites
To the eyes of the Boer, who believed in the superiority of his race, the sight of white men reduced to the level of natives was horrifying. The spectacle of poor white slums could not be tolerated. They had no education or resources but because they had the vote they had an enormous political influence.
(Parker & Pfukani, 'Southern Africa', Bell & Hyman, 1984.)

SOURCE 49 — National Party Legislation
Hertzog enacted his 'Colour Bar' Bill, the Mines and Works Amendment Act of 1926 which barred Africans from a variety of better paid jobs whatever their skills. He strengthened the Masters and Servants Act and dealt with the influx of Africans (in) towns by even stricter segregation and discriminatory laws.
(Mary Benson, 'Struggle for a Birthright', IDAF, 1985, p. 48.)

In the 1930s, following the Wall Street Crash, the economic problems of South Africa worsened. To try and solve the problems Hertzog and Smuts joined their two parties and formed the United Party. The more extreme nationalists said that coalition with Smuts was a betrayal of Afrikaner ideals and left to form a 'purified' National Party. The leader of this new group was Daniel Malan. In the elections of 1938 the new party gained a respectable 27 seats. The more moderate ideas of Smuts and Hertzog had less and less appeal to the ordinary Afrikaner.

When war broke out in 1939 opinion in South Africa was again divided. A small majority in Parliament voted to fight for Britain. Hertzog, who had spoken out against the First World War, was again opposed to war with Germany. He left the coalition and joined forces with Malan. The cause of Afrikaner Nationalism was again united, but Malan saw himself as the real leader of the Afrikaner nation.

The poor whites. The poverty facing many Afrikaners in the 1920s and 1930s was an important issue in South African politics.

Questions
1. How did the problem of the poor whites and the way the Afrikaner was treated contribute to the growing popularity of the National Party?
2. What problems revealed in Sources 47 and 48 horrified Afrikaner Nationalists? Why would they be so horrified at the details revealed in the sources?
3. From reading Source 49 explain why Afrikaner Nationalists would have approved of Hertzog's policies.
4. How significant was the growing popularity of the National Party?

The Broederbond

This chapter deals with the following topics:
1. The formation of the Broederbond.
2. The work of the Broederbond.
3. The influence of the Broederbond.
4. Extreme Afrikaner Nationalism and Nazi Germany.

After you have read this chapter and completed the exercises you will have:
1. Discovered the part played by the Broederbond in South Africa.
2. Understood the part played by groups like the Broederbond in South Africa.

Broederbond is an Afrikaans word that means 'band of brothers'. This very secretive and shadowy organisation has, over the years, had a powerful influence in South African politics and society. Prime Ministers, politicians and businessmen have been and still are members, though few admit they are Broeders.

The Broederbond was formed in 1918 with the aim of preserving the Afrikaner's culture and his way of life. English was still the dominant language and the members of the Broederbond were worried that English culture would swamp the Afrikaner. Some of the earliest members were teachers; the Broederbond placed a great deal of importance on education as a means of preserving the Afrikaans language.

The greatest achievement of the Broederbond was re-enacting the Great Trek in 1938. Afrikaners set out from Cape Town dressed in the costume of the 1830s, complete with covered wagons pulled by oxen. The Trek was a great success. Thousands turned out to greet the Trekkers in every town and village on the route to Pretoria. It made Afrikaners proud of their history and the hardships faced by their ancestors. When they reached the outskirts of Pretoria, to lay the foundations of the Voortrekker Monument, there was a huge rally. The mood was fiercely patriotic. Alan Paton, a South African writer, said that it was a lonely and terrible occasion for any English-speaking South African.

SOURCE 50 — The British and the Afrikaner

There was a Nationalist Party meeting in Johannesburg on Saturday 13th April 1918. The main speaker was Daniel Malan. It would have been normal for the Union Jack to have been displayed in the hall but a small group of people quietly removed the flag and put it aside.

A large crowd of English speakers, having heard about the flag, gathered outside the hall singing patriotic songs and spoiling for a fight. When the Nationalist audience left the hall there was a free-for-all in the street. Then the English mob moved up the street to the unguarded Nationalist Club. The crowd broke in, carried the

furniture out into the street and set it alight. Then from the balcony they flew the Union Jack. Later, for good measure, they set fire to the building as well.
(Harrison, op. cit., p. 84.)

SOURCE 51 — The Aims of the Broederbond

◄ What were the aims of the Broederbond?

Our aim was to develop an organisation in which Afrikaners could find each other and be able to work together for the survival of the Afrikaner people in South Africa and the promotion of its interests.
(Henning Klopper, first Chairman of the Broederbond.)

The Broederbond: The Role of Groups and Personalities

SOURCE 52 — Re-enacting the Great Trek 1938

We prayed that the symbolic Trek we were about to re-enact would bring Afrikaners together. We ask the entire Afrikanerdom to take part in the festival in this spirit. We long that nothing shall hinder the Afrikaner people as a whole from taking part. This movement comes from the people; may the people carry it in their hearts all the way to Pretoria and Blood River.

Let us build up a monument for Afrikaner hearts. May this simple Trek bind together in love those Afrikaner hearts which do not yet beat together. We dedicate these wagons to our people and our God.
(Henning Klopper's address to the Trek before it left Cape Town in August 1938.)

Troops of the Ossewa Brandwag. Their uniforms and military training and their extreme Nationalist views brought comparison with Hitler's Storm-Troopers in Germany.

SOURCE 53 — The Ossewa Brandwag and the Second World War

They (the Ossewa Brandwag) went under a bridge and they had their dynamite there to blow up the bridge just before the train came. But, and I wouldn't say unfortunately, they blew themselves up. Had they succeeded they would not have blown up the troop train but the train of families who were going to Durban to say goodbye.

The 1938 Trek was a great success for the Nationalists. Thousands of Afrikaners were reminded of their heroic ancestors. Not since the time of the Boer War were they so united. Many felt that the time had come to cut the links with the British Empire and set up an independent Republic. Some anti-British nationalists formed the Ossewa Brandwag, the Ox-Wagon Brigade. This was almost a military organisation; the members had military ranks and wore uniforms. The Ossewa Brandwag was for white supremacy and violently anti-Jewish. A Jewish trade union leader, Solly Sachs, was told that Nazi Germany would seem like a Jewish paradise compared to South Africa if the Ossewa Brandwag had its way. They saw themselves as protectors and, if necessary, fighters for the rights of the Afrikaner.

In the Second World War the Ossewa Brandwag and many right-wing Afrikaners supported Hitler. This was not surprising as some Ossewa Brandwag leaders had studied in Nazi Germany. The military parades and the anti-Jewish policies of the Ossewa Brandwag were copied from the Nazis. Several of the leaders of the Ossewa Brandwag were thought to be a threat to South Africa during the war and were imprisoned; among them was J. B. Vorster, who became Prime Minister of South Africa in 1966.

SOURCE 54 — The influence of the Broederbond in post-war South Africa
1. The Afrikaner Broederbond, with its fanatical racial aims and with its offspring, the Ossewa Brandwag, has become a formidable subversive force.
2. The parent is much more dangerous than the child. The Ossewa Brandwag sprang up only because the ground had been prepared for it by the Broederbond. Its leaders have been in close contact with the Nazis and have copied their methods wholesale.
3. The Ossewa Brandwag will wane with the Nazis. The Broederbond will outlive both because its policy is much more patient. The Broederbond is a malignant cancer in South Africa and only the knife can remove it.
4. The Broederbond has obtained a stranglehold on education which will enable it to govern South Africa within a few decades. Some thousands of civil servants and teachers are bound by oath to carry out the plans of the Broederbond.
(Report made by Ernie Malherbe, Head of South African Intelligence during the war. 'The White Tribe of Africa' by David Harrison, BBC Publications, 1981.)

The Broederbond: The influence of personalities and groups

In the years since 1948 the Broederbond has continued to exert a powerful influence in South Africa. In the most important positions of public life in South Africa the Broederbond is still very powerful. The majority of Nationalist politicians are Broeders; most directors of the South African Broadcasting Corporation and many editors of newspapers which support the government are members of the Broederbond. In education the Broederbond has been successful in getting Afrikaner ideas into the classroom. Most history lessons have a Nationalist bias and the majority of teachers are Afrikaners.

Daniel Malan's government in 1948. All but two of the cabinet ministers were senior members of the Broederbond.

SOURCE 55 — The Broederbond's Influence

At the height of its power in the 1950s and 1960s few senior appointments went to people who were not Broeders. All South Africa's Prime Ministers have been Broeders. The Broeders dominate the National Party, the South African Broadcasting Corporation, the Dutch Reformed Church, local councils, the civil service, the police and defence forces, sports bodies, universities, Afrikaans newspapers and so on. The result is that within fifty years political and economic power was in the hands of the Afrikaners and was controlled by the Broederbond through the ruling National Party.

(Graham Leach 'South Africa', Methuen 1987, p. 109.)

Afrikaners are divided about the present reforms which the government is supposed to be introducing. In recent years a small but noisy group, the Afrikaner Resistance Movement (the AWB), has made a spectacular appearance in South Africa. They feel that the reforms of P. W. Botha threaten the traditional Afrikaner way of life. The AWB members wear military-style uniforms and have an emblem similar to the swastika. Their leader, Eugène Terre Blanche, has been found guilty of illegally possessing arms; other members of the AWB have been imprisoned for plotting to kill Bishop Tutu.

SOURCE 56 — The AWB
Pietersburg, northern Transvaal, 22 May 1986
Several hundred Afrikaner whites stormed a hall in this conservative town to prevent Foreign Minister Pik Botha from addressing a public meeting. The AWB leader Eugène Terre Blanche is carried shoulder high by his supporters, a man with a calling to save white South Africa. Police tried to restore order by using tear gas and many were injured in a free for all. The meeting was abandoned in chaos.
(Graham Leach, 'South Africa', Methuen, 1987, p. 99.)

Questions

1. How does Source 50 show that some Afrikaners thought there was a need to protect the Afrikaner way of life? Is there any reason why the British crowd should have reacted the way they did? (The date is significant here.)

2. From Source 52: How important was the Centenary Trek for Afrikaner Nationalism?

3. Were there any similarities between the Ossewa Brandwag and the Nazi Party in Germany?

4. Ernie Malherbe thought that the Broederbond was more dangerous than the Ossewa Brandwag. Do Sources 53 and 54 confirm these views?

5. Smuts blamed his election defeat on the Broederbond. Was this true? Does the picture on page 31 help you to answer this question?

6. How important has the Broederbond been in shaping South Africa since 1948?

7. Are there any similarities between the Ossewa Brandwag and the AWB? Are there any factors responsible for the popularity of the AWB which were also responsible for the growth of the Ossewa Brandwag in the 1930s?

Separate Development

This chapter deals with the following topics:
1. The election of the Nationalist Party in 1948 and the introduction of apartheid.
2. The Population Registration Act and the Prohibition of Mixed Marriages Act.
3. The effects of these laws on the non-white population.

After reading this chapter and completing the exercises you will have:
1. Seen that the election in 1948 was a turning point in South African history.
2. Discovered the consequences of apartheid laws.

In the election campaign of 1948 Malan's National Party promised to look after the interests of the white population. Their policy was summed up in one word: **apartheid,** an Afrikaans word which means 'apartness'. Their aim was total separation of the races. Another Afrikaner politician was more blunt; he described apartheid as boss-ship or domination. The election was a turning-point — the National Party has remained the party of government for forty years, its policies receiving the support of the majority of white South Africans.

The policy of apartheid was also a turning-point in South African history. Earlier laws limited the rights of the non-white population, but those introduced after 1948 gradually affected every aspect of life. South Africans, white and black, were to live in certain areas, were not free to marry whom they liked. Education, employment, social services and health services were all part of the apartheid state. Even the right to call yourself a South African depended not on where you were born, but on the colour of your skin.

The first apartheid laws were the Population Registration Act and the Prohibition of Mixed Marriages Act, which divided the entire population of South Africa into racial groups and made it an offence to marry and later to have any sexual relations with persons from another racial group.

SOURCE 57 — Discrimination before 1948

The 1913 Natives Land Act forced hundreds of thousands of Africans off farms they had bought and forced them into reserves for Africans only. The reserves amounted to some 13 per cent of the land of South Africa.

The Mines and Works Act reserved jobs for certain races and made strikes by black workers illegal. In 1936 Cape Africans were taken off the electoral roll and lost their right to vote in the same elections as whites.
(Roger Omond 'The Apartheid Handbook', Penguin Books, 1986.)

SOURCE 58 — The Population Registration Act 1950

The register of the population of the Republic of South Africa prepared by the Secretary of the Interior contains all the names of all South African citizens, classified as white, African, Asian or Coloured as the case may be.

Every person over the age of 16 must possess an identity card which includes a photograph and describes him as a white person, a Coloured person, or an African and, when the holder is an African, it must state in addition the ethnic group or tribe to which he belongs.
('Apartheid in Practice', United Nations Publications, 1976.)

SOURCE 59 — The Morality Laws

Marriages between whites and Coloured persons, Asians or Africans are prohibited. If a marriage officer performs a marriage ceremony between a white man and a Coloured woman, for example, the marriage is void.
(Prohibition of Mixed Marriages Act, 1949.)

A man, whether married or single, who is a white person and who attempts to have sexual intercourse with a woman who is not white is guilty of a criminal offence, punishable by imprisonment with compulsory hard labour for up to seven years.

The Immorality Act 1957.
('Apartheid in Practice', United Nations Publications, 1976.)

◀ Using Sources 57, 58 and 59 do you find that the Nationalist election victory brought about
a. a change in racial policies *or*
b. a continuation with similar racial policies?

Question
What do you understand by the term 'Apartheid'?

Separate Development: A Turning Point

To Afrikaner political and religious leaders the Mixed Marriages Act and the Immorality Acts were an important part of apartheid. They often explained the laws in religious terms, but in truth all they wanted was to retain the 'purity' and the superiority of white South Africa. There are many similarities between the South African morality laws and the Nuremberg Laws that the Nazis introduced in Germany in 1935. The National Party justified the laws by claiming to remove sources of friction between the different groups. It was better to separate and have as little contact as possible. However, a prominent government figure, J. Strijdom, said that the National Party stood for 'Baaskap' (boss-ship) or domination by the whites of non-white South Africans.

SOURCE 60 — Deciding Racial Grouping

White officials were known to use the 'pencil in the hair' technique. If a pencil pushed into the hair of the applicant stayed there because the hair was crinkly, then he was put down as African; if it fell out because the hair was straighter, then he was Coloured.

SOURCE 61 — The Dutch Reformed Church and the Morality Laws

We felt very strongly that we had to preserve our identity, because that is a God given right that every man has. God created us differently, and it is to the honour of God that we must preserve that difference. We felt so strongly that God gave man the Ten Commandments and one of them said 'Honour thy father and mother'. That means it is not just a matter of obeying your parents. You must also honour your parents by preserving their identity.
(Koot Vorster Dominee (Leader) of the Dutch Reformed Church. David Harrison, 'The White Tribe of Africa', BBC Publications, 1981, p. 158-57.)

◄ How did the Afrikaners justify their morality laws?
◄ On what grounds could these laws be criticised?

Separate Development: The Consequences of the Morality Laws

The Morality Laws and the Population Registration Act are all written in legal and impersonal language. It is easy to forget that such laws were applied to real people. Laws designed to make people feel inferior cause anger; elsewhere the workings of the law resulted in personal tragedy.

Joyce Sikakane was a resident of Soweto on the outskirts of Johannesburg. When she left school she had to 'register' for a Pass before she could start work.

Under the Pass Laws (Section 10) there were four categories of lawful residence in any African urban area. Those were:
1. To be born there.
2. To have worked for 10 years or lived for 15 years under certain conditions.
3. To be the wife or child of a person qualified under (1.).
4. To have a work permit and accommodation.

Joyce Sikakane, resident of Soweto, but now living in exile.

SOURCE 62 — The Population Registration Act

I was a Section Tenner having been born in Soweto, and being the daughter of a man who was also qualified. At the Labour Bureau a white official wanted proof that I was entitled to be in Soweto. The only proof that I thought of was my father's Pass Book. But then he did not have time to come to the office with me. He had to be at work. He could not dream of giving me his Pass in case anything happened to it. Besides it would mean arrest by the cops if he failed to produce it. Finally he decided to risk it and gave me his pass. I was not to leave it at the Labour Office. On the following day I ran most of the two miles distance to the Labour Office. When my turn came, I showed the labour officer my father's pass. In it was stated where he was born and that he was a registered house tenant and employee. The official took down notes and gave me the stinker (an African expression for a Pass Book) back. Despite this documentary proof, he had to check with Pretoria before granting me permission to register as an employed 'Bantu' female. I waited three months for clearance. You can imagine my anxiety in case I was endorsed out of Johannesburg. Finally I got the labour stamp of a Section Tenner. I was officially a desirable 'Bantu' female.
(Joyce Sikakane, 'Window on Soweto', IDAF Publications, 1976.)

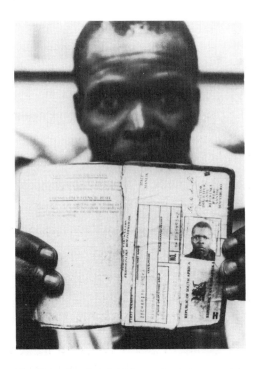

The Pass Book. All Africans had to carry this document. Failure to do so was a criminal offence. The Pass not only showed an African's name but where he worked and lived. Details in the Pass had to be brought up to date regularly.

◀ Using Source 58 and the picture above, can you explain why the Population Registration Act was disliked by many non-white South Africans?

A family of mixed race. The problems which the Mixed Marriages Act and the Group Areas Act created for families such as this were enormous. Legally people from the 'wrong' race were not allowed to live in certain city suburbs. A brother could find himself classified coloured, while his sister might be registered as a white South African.

The Mixed Marriages Act is probably one of the most controversial pieces of apartheid law. Before the law was passed there were very few instances of mixed marriages — less than one hundred a year. For the people affected the problems can be distressing. Children in the same family can find that they are put into different race groups. In a country where housing, jobs and education are decided on grounds of race the problems faced by mixed race families can be tragic.

SOURCE 63 — The effects of the Prohibition of Mixed Marriages Act

Raymond du Proft was a Belgian born white South African. In 1950 just after the government introduced its Mixed Marriages Act he was serving in the police force. He was twenty when he met Diane Bassick who was working in a Cape Town restaurant. They fell in love but since she was classified Coloured they could only meet in secret.

Before long they took a chance and started to live together. When their first son was born six years later they found a house in an Afrikaans speaking district and passed themselves off without any difficulty as a white married couple. Eventually they had five children, all of whom were classified as Coloured. Under the Nationalist law they should have gone to a school for Coloureds in a different district. To maintain the pretence of being white the du Profts kept the children at home and educated them as best they could. Regularly they applied for Diane and the children to be re-classified white and just as regularly they were refused. Marriage remained out of the question. When their eldest son, Graham, was nineteen he started going out with an Afrikaans speaking girl and she became pregnant. But again because he was classified Coloured and she was white they could not marry. In a moment of despair, Graham threw himself under a train; he died instantly.

(David Harrison, 'The White Tribe of Africa', BBC Publications, 1981, p. 161-62.)

Questions
1. A Pass Book was much more than an identity card. How does Source 62 prove this statement?
2. Using Source 62 can you say how the Pass Law affects the lives of Africans living in urban areas?
3. In what ways was the Prohibition of Mixed Marriages Act a heartless law?

The Land

This chapter deals with the following topics:
1. The Native Land Acts of 1913 and 1936.
2. The Land Policies of the National Party.
3. The Group Areas Act.
4. The Social Effects of the Group Areas Act.

After reading this chapter and completing the exercises you will have:
1. Discovered the reasons for the passing of the Land Acts.
2. Examined the similarities between the earlier Land Acts and the Group Areas Act.
3. Seen how the Homelands Policy was a turning point in the idea of apartheid.
4. Looked at the importance of the Homelands Policy in the 1980s.

In 1913 the government passed the Natives Land Act. This set down the areas in South Africa where Africans were allowed to own land and live. The Africans were given 7 per cent of the land; the remaining 93 per cent was for whites. Land for Africans was in such short supply that they could no longer follow their traditional way of life. When they tried to farm the land it quickly became exhausted and eroded.

To support their families African men were forced to leave the land and their families to work in the mines. Others worked with their families on white farms. They were not paid and had to work for the white farmer for 90 days. In return they were allowed to keep a few animals and grow crops. Africans in the Natives National Congress protested. Some even travelled to London in an attempt to interest the British government in their plight. Their objections came to nothing.

In 1936 a further Native Land Act was passed which gave the Africans more land. They were now legally entitled to 13 per cent of the land. Many whites opposed this proposal. They argued that the Africans had enough land under the 1913 Act. They were speaking for the white farmers who might lose land. Almost as compensation, the Africans living on white farms now had to work 180 days.

SOURCE 64 — The effects of the Land Acts

The chief enemy of the African people was, and still is today, the Land Act of 1913. It caused starvation because the breadwinner would leave the country to provide the big farmers of South Africa with cheap labour.

My parents wanted to come here because it was safe for them to work on their own land rather than to work for the whites. They wanted to live peacefully not under the permission of anybody.

◄ How did the Land Acts of 1913 and 1936 affect the Africans?

After my father bought the land what he grows on the land is maize and beans. It was enough to feed himself and his family and what remains he can sell to other people. It was much better than working in Johannesburg because that is no place for his children to live a proper life. So he thought that it would be better to buy his own place where he would live with his family.
(Africans describing how the Land Acts affected their families. In the second paragraph the African's father had bought the land before 1913.)

The Group Areas Act: A Turning Point

The Natives Land Acts had only applied to the African population; in 1950 the Group Areas Act was passed and applied to all South Africans. The aim of this Act was to establish areas where each racial group would live. The National Party said that this would prevent trouble between different racial groups. Towns and cities were to be zoned. Each group would only be allowed to live in the areas set aside for them. Overnight, Africans, Asians and Coloureds were living in the wrong area. These people found that they were to be forcibly moved from areas where they had been living for many years. Very few whites were affected by the Group Areas Act.

The most notorious of these forced removals took place in Sophiatown, a suburb of Johannesburg. Sophiatown was a unique area in South Africa. For almost 50 years Africans, Asians, Coloureds and a few whites had lived peacefully together. Sophiatown was living proof that all races in South Africa could live together. In spite of popular protests the Africans were evicted, their few belongings put on to trucks and dumped in the new African locations on the South West of Johannesburg. Their homes were flattened by bulldozers and the people moved, some to Soweto, while others were given tents and dumped in the open countryside.

SOURCE 65 — Sophiatown

Sophiatown is a happy place. It has a life about it which belongs to no other suburb in South Africa. It positively sparkles. Sophiatown is a community which has grown through the years. Xosa and Motswans (African tribes), Indian and Chinese, coloured and white have all contributed something to it. The place is cosmopolitan. You can go into a store to buy a packet of cigarettes and be served by a Chinaman or an Indian. An 'American' barber's shop stands next door to an African herbalist's store. White South Africa has written off Sophiatown as a slum area; its values must be those of the slum; its people must be dirty, undesirable and, above all unseen.

The issue was dead simple. It was just this: that white Johannesburg had encroached on black Johannesburg, and so, naturally, black Johannesburg must move on. An African township, established for 50 years, can be uprooted and totally destroyed because it is next to a European suburb. If a black township stands where a white suburb wants to stand, the township must go. The plain truth is that the Government's scheme was not slum clearance but robbery: robbery carried out under pressure from the neighbouring white suburbs.
('Naught for Your Comfort', by Trevor Huddleston, Collins, 1956.)

Sophiatown grew up as a multi-racial suburb of Johannesburg. It was one of the few areas where Africans had been able to buy their own houses. The government claimed that the area was a slum, others said that Sophiatown was living proof that all races in South Africa could live together.

SOURCE 66 — The End of Sophiatown

The removal had begun, a whole fleet of army lorries was drawn up. Lining the street were thousands of police armed with rifles. The lorries were piled high with the pathetic possessions. A rusty kitchen stove; a few blackened pots and pans; a wicker chair, mattresses; bundles of heaven knows what, and people, soaked, all soaked to the skin by the drenching rain. The first lorries began to move away to Meadowlands eight miles to the west. 60,000 people removed to Meadowlands, a living community destroyed.

'But after all Father Huddleston,' said a BBC reporter, 'you must admit that Sophiatown was a slum. And I've seen Meadowlands: it's fine, they're quite happy. Do you think all the fuss was a bit of a mistake?'

To me it seems that white South Africa thinks that an African in the kraal is in his right place: so is the African in the kitchen. But the African in a 'European' suburb, in a European house which he owns and is proud of: he is a menace and must be removed.
(From 'Naught for Your Comfort', by Trevor Huddleston, Collins, 1956.)

Questions

1. According to Source 64 why did some Africans prefer to buy small farms rather than work in Johannesburg?
2. If the farm in Source 64 was not in the area of a Native Reserve what would have happened to the farmer?
3. What did Bishop Huddleston think was unique about Sophiatown?
4. Does your answer to Question 3 suggest any reasons why the government might want to remove the population of Sophiatown?
5. In what ways were the Sophiatown Evictions a consequence of the Group Areas Act?
6. What arguments were used by the government in Source 66 to justify the removals? How might Bishop Huddleston reply to such arguments?

The Land: The Homelands Policy

The Homelands are those areas which the Africans were given under the Land Acts of 1913 and 1936. These areas were the 'Reserves'. After the election of the Nationalists in 1948 there was a change of policy towards the Homelands. The Minister for Bantu Affairs, Hendrik Verwoerd, wanted the Homelands to become self-ruling independent black nations. This was the policy of Grand Apartheid. All Africans would become citizens of one of the Homelands. Africans would only be able to live in white areas as long as they were working. The Nationalists tried to present this policy as more humane; they began to call their policy 'Separate Development'. These Homelands were first called Bantustans; later they were given names like Transkei, Ciskei and Bophutatswana to make them sound like separate nations.

SOURCE 67 — Nationalist politicians justify the Homelands Policy

When I talk of the nation of South Africa, I talk of the white people. I do not see us as one multi-racial state descended from various groups. We are eliminating the friction between different racial groups.
(Hendrik Verwoerd.)

The Bantu Self Government Act is bringing to fruition the African's personal and national ideals within his own ethnic group. We grant to the Bantu what we demand for ourselves — independence.

I really thought that it would work, that we could have happy prosperous Homelands developing into independent republics. Most of the Blacks would be sheltered there and find an income there while we, the whites, in the rest of South Africa might be able to manage our own affairs.

All the Bantu have their permanent home in the reserves and their entry into the urban areas is only temporary and for economic reasons. They are admitted as work seekers not as settlers. As soon as they become no longer fit for work they are expected to return to Homeland where they fit in. Even if they were not born or bred in the Homeland.

SOURCE 68 — Conditions in the Homelands

An inquiry into the living conditions in the Reserves reveals that the inhabitants find it impossible to supply even the bare necessities for living on a subsistence level. Opportunities for jobs are almost non-existent. There is evidence of malnutrition. Disease is rife in many areas.

The easier the living in the Reserves, the less labour is available for outside employment. The temptation for Europeans not to improve the living has always been strong. The demand for labour has usually decided the issue.
(Piet Koornhof, an Afrikaner politician writing about the Reserves in 1953.)

◀ What was the Homelands Policy?

The Homelands Policy: A Change in the Idea of Apartheid

Before the Homelands were set up the government appointed a Commission of Inquiry led by Professor Tomlinson. The Commission had to look at conditions in the Reserves and recommend ways in which they could become independent. The Tomlinson Commission took four years to gather its evidence and the report was a massive 17 volumes. It suggested ways in which the Reserves could become separate independent states. The government only accepted the parts of the Report which it agreed with.

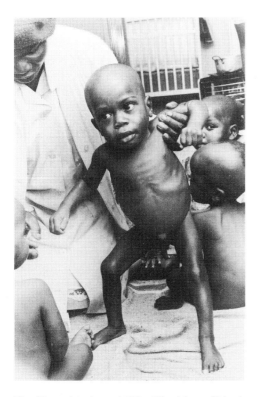

The Homelands — 1980s. The idea of black Homelands was an attempt to sell apartheid to the world. Dr Verwoerd called it a policy of 'good neighbourliness'. Overcrowding, exhausted land and a deliberate decision not to invest in the development of the Homelands has created 'Third World' areas in a First World nation. The photograph shows a child suffering from the effects of malnutrition. This is one of the largest killers of children under the age of five in the Homelands.

SOURCE 69 — The conclusions of the Tomlinson Report
1. The Reserves were overpopulated and agriculture could not feed the people. Jobs had to be found and agriculture improved.
2. More land would have to be set aside and industry established both in the Reserves and on the borders.
3. Such development, providing about 50,000 jobs a year, would, with other improvements, cost 104 million Rand over a ten-year period.
4. The Reserves should be concentrated into seven 'Bantustans' corresponding with the major tribal divisions.

SOURCE 70 — Conditions in the Homelands
In the children's ward at a hospital in Nondweni, Kwazulu, half of all the children admitted were underweight. Diseases due to poor diet, like kwashiorkor, were commonplace. In 1980 more than 50 children died from malnutrition, half of all child deaths in the hospital. With no room to plant, with no cattle to provide meat or milk, the Zulus of Nondweni declined. There was virtually no work. The able-bodied men had to leave and seek work elsewhere. Tomlinson had recommended that the area could support about 13,000 people; in 1979 the population was around 200,000.
('The White Tribe of Africa', by David Harrison, BBC Publications, 1981.)

SOURCE 71 — Black reaction to the Homelands
It was never considered that these 'Reserves' could become economically self-sufficient national homes. The Reserves are distressed areas unable to support their present populations. The majority of the adult males are always away from home working in the mines or European farms. The government have no intention of creating African areas which are self-supporting. If such areas were self-supporting where would the mine owners and the farmers get their supplies of cheap labour? The miserly 500,000 Rand voted to the Bantu Investment Corporation is mere eyewash: it would not build a single decent road, railway line or power station.
('Verwoerd's Tribalism', by Nelson Mandela in 'The Struggle is My Life', IDAF Publications, 1986.)

Chapter 8

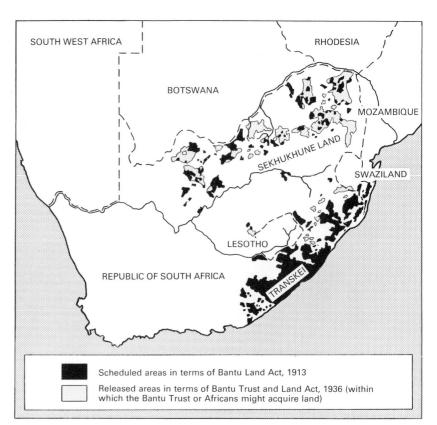

The Native Land Acts set aside areas of South Africa where Africans could legally buy land and settle. The Native Reserves tended to be in the poorest parts of the country where land was poor and there were few mineral resources. The 1913 Act set aside only 7 per cent of the land for Africans.

Legend for map:

- Scheduled areas in terms of Bantu Land Act, 1913
- Released areas in terms of Bantu Trust and Land Act, 1936 (within which the Bantu Trust or Africans might acquire land)

Landscape of the Homelands.

Questions

1. In Source 67 some of the speakers talk about giving Africans freedom in their own land. Does the final speaker in Source 67 confirm that this was the aim of the Homelands policy?
2. How might the Tomlinson Commission have raised living standards in the Homelands?
3. From Sources 68 and 70 what effects did the Tomlinson Commission have on conditions in the Homelands? Can Tomlinson be blamed for this?
4. What did the author of Source 71 think of the Reserves? Can you explain his point of view?
5. How true were his criticisms of the Homelands policy?

The Land: The Present Day Importance

Hendrik Verwoerd was proud of the Homelands policy. He saw it as a way of solving South Africa's problems. Overnight, Africans became citizens of their tribal Homelands even if they had never lived there. As citizens of the Homelands there was no justification for demanding equality or voting rights in South Africa. To look at a map of the Homelands reveals what an artificial creation they are. Bophuthatswana consists of six islands in white South Africa.

For Africans living in towns there was always the risk of being 'Endorsed Out'. If an African lost his job or his home he could be forced out of the Township where he might have been living for many years. Suddenly the entire family might have to move to a Homeland. If he eventually found work he faced the problem of becoming a migrant worker, returning to his family for a few weeks each year.

The rulers of such Homelands are regarded as traitors by many of their fellow Africans. In Transkei, the first independent Homeland, Chief Kaiser Matanzima was appointed leader. The citizens of Transkei voted against Matanzima in the Parliamentary elections, but with the support of the other Chiefs he became Prime Minister. Family and friends were given top jobs and corruption was rife.

In South Africa the leaders of the Homelands are treated as important heads of state by the government. The Homelands are not economically self-sufficient and could not exist without money from South Africa. African Nationalists in South Africa treat the leaders of the Homelands with contempt. The leader of Kwa Zulu, Chief Buthelezi, has refused the offer of independence. He realises that it would be a false independence and does nothing to solve the real problems of South Africa. Not one country recognises the Homelands and all insist they are part of South Africa.

The forced removals from both urban and rural areas to remove 'Black Spots' and tidy up the racial picture of South Africa have been widely criticised. The government of South Africa realises that removals provoke strong foreign criticism and claims to have halted any more forced removals. Between 1960 and 1983 over 3,500,000 removals had taken place and there are still around 2,000,000 people living in the 'wrong area'. However, despite official claims, people are still being encouraged to move to the correct location.

SOURCE 72 — The scale of forced removals
The exact total is not known. The best estimate was made in 1983 by a team of researchers known as the Surplus People Project. It said that between 1960 and 1983 a total of 3,522,900 removals had taken place. According to the Project, another 1,800,000 people are under threat of removal.

The main removal groups are:
Eviction of black tenants from farms.
Clearing black-owned property outside Homelands.
Moving townships in white areas to Homelands.
Under the Group Areas Act in cities.

Chapter 8

Three-quarters of those moved were Africans. A total of 2,262 white families were moved under the Group Areas Act.
('The Apartheid Handbook', Roger Omond, Penguin Books, 1986.)

Forced eviction. This photograph was taken at the Crossroads Squatter Camp on the outskirts of Cape Town in May 1986. It shows an African woman walking away from the ruins of her house with a sheet of corrugated iron. In the background is a bulldozer demolishing what was once her family home. The squatters were illegally occupying land and scenes like this have been repeated all over South Africa since the passing of the Group Areas Act of 1950.

SOURCE 73 — The reality of removal

Reserve Six was allocated to the majority black population in 1913. It is a glorious stretch of green land up the coast from Durban. In 1976 the Government moved about 6,000 blacks living there to a re-settlement point at Ntambanana.

A white farmer who went broke trying to make a living there said of it:
'It's dry thorn country with not one permanent stream. The soil is shallow and infertile.'

Today the contrast is dramatic. In what was Reserve Six there are white areas with street names like Geranium Place. I watched a weary looking black woman pushing an ice-cream cart summoned by a little boy who came running over a green lawn to buy an ice-cream. In Ntambanana I watched children his age struggling up hills carrying plastic containers and pushing them in barrows hunting for water. In that area swarming with children the only shop for miles did not have a single sweet.
(The Guardian, 8 August 1986.)

Over the years the government has carried out a series of forced removals from 'Black spots'. People evicted have been moved to the Homelands where the only buildings waiting for them were rows of corrugated iron toilet shacks.

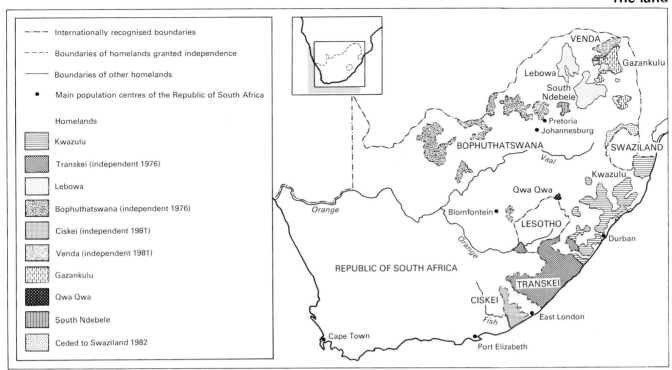

The Homelands. These were set up as a result of Verwoerd's Bantu Self Government Act. The areas set aside for the Homelands were similar to those lands which had been given their independence. Bophuthatswana is made up of several 'islands' surrounded by white South Africa.

SOURCE 74 — Squatters

The Pass Laws prevent wives and families of migrant workers from living with them: for this reason and to escape worse poverty in the homelands, families have often built makeshift accommodation near or in African townships. Conditions in the squatter camps are often very bad. In 1983, 900 odd people were in the Nyanga dunes living in tents and plastic bag shelters. Some 300 had had no toilets for three months or more.

('The Apartheid Handbook', Roger Omond, Penguin Books, 1986.)

SOURCE 75 — Crossroads Camp near Cape Town

Crossroads is in many ways a symbol of the apartheid system. Here in defiance of the homelands policy and the Group Areas Act and of many attempts to forcibly remove them, thousands of families have chosen to squat. When we visited the community it was sticking together. Its families were crowded into crude shanties, fashioned from discarded sheets of corrugated iron and lined with cardboard and polythene in an attempt to keep out the cold. The shanties have neither sewage system nor electricity and only a few communal water taps. Yet the people were clean, the shacks generally tidy.

('Mission To South Africa', by the Commonwealth Eminent Persons Group, Penguin Books, 1986.)

Questions

1. Sources 65 and 66 describe the Sophiatown evictions. This was just one example of the working of the Group Areas Act. On what sort of scale did the Group Areas Act work?
2. Using Source 73 can you suggest why some forced removals have taken place? From reading this source do you think all South Africans are equally affected by these laws?
3. What is illegal about the settlements described in Sources 74 and 75?
4. Why are so many South Africans willing to break the law by living in a place like Crossroads? How might residents of Crossroads justify breaking the law?
5. Why has the government promised to end forced removals and halted evictions at places like Crossroads?

The Law

This chapter deals with the following topics:

1. The growth of opposition to apartheid.
2. The introduction of laws to silence opposition to apartheid.
3. How these laws have affected the opponents of apartheid.
4. The death of Steve Biko.

After reading this chapter and completing the exercises you will have:

1. Discovered the consequences of opposition to apartheid.
2. Examined the conflicting evidence surrounding the death of Steve Biko.

Since 1948, Nationalist governments have introduced a series of harsh laws to enforce apartheid. Some of the laws appear unusual to us in Britain and they make petty criminals out of ordinary law-abiding people. They were the Pass Laws. Every non-white South African had, until recently, to carry a Pass Book. The pass contains a wealth of information about its holder. All blacks over the age of sixteen had to carry a pass and to be caught without it was a criminal offence. It is estimated that around **two million** people have been arrested since 1975 for Pass Law offences. Pass Laws were an important weapon in the government's campaign to stop illegal entry into urban areas. Without the right stamp in a Pass Book it can be illegal to live in a township, it can be impossible to get work. An African runs the risk of being ordered out of a township back to a Homeland.

One of the first laws that the Nationalists passed on coming to power was the Suppression of Communism Act. The Communist party was outlawed and membership became a criminal offence. This has become a law with very wide powers. A communist does not actually have to be a member of the Communist Party; the Minister of Justice decides who is a communist. It has been said that in South Africa a communist is anyone who disagrees with the government.

SOURCE 76 — The Pass Laws

On Maundy Thursday night, Jacob Ledwaba had been arrested for being out after the curfew and without his pass. On Saturday morning he came home. If you are an African and you have left your pass at home, you have committed a crime: you can be arrested and imprisoned and the quickest and safest way to get your release is to pay an admission of guilt fine without argument. The fact that you are not guilty of any real offence is beside the point. You are an offender because by accident, you have tried to evade the control of the state and it is the duty of the police to remind you of the fact. ('Naught for your Comfort', by Trevor Huddleston, Fontana, 1956.)

SOURCE 77 — Why the Afrikaner dislikes communists

Communism recognises no distinctions of race. At meetings of the Communist Party White, Black and Brown persons sit together. At socials they drink tea together and at dances the Black native whirls with his arm around the waist of the White girl. What follows? The effect of communism was quickly visible in the impertinent attitudes of natives towards Europeans.
(Pamphlet, 'The Communist Danger', by Eric Louw.)

SOURCE 78 — Who is a Communist?

A Communist for the terms of the Act is:
A person who belongs to the Communist Party or who believes in the ideas of Karl Marx or Lenin.

Any person who commits any act which is likely, in the opinion of the Minister of Justice, to encourage hostility between members of the European and non-European races.

Any person who wants to bring about any social change in the Republic of South Africa by unlawful acts.

While the Suppression of Communism Act made the Communist Party illegal its wide definition of a Communist has made it a difficult law to enforce. Very few people have been successfully prosecuted under this law.
(In 'The Rise of the South African Reich', by Brian Bunting, IDAF Publications, Reprinted 1986.)

The Law: A Consequence of Apartheid

As opposition to apartheid grew in the 1950s the government passed a series of laws aimed at making protest difficult. People convicted under the Terrorism Act or the Internal Security Act face lengthy terms of imprisonment and in some cases the death penalty. These laws have been used against Trade Union leaders, the leaders of political parties or anyone who speaks out against apartheid. People arrested can be held in detention for up to 180 days for questioning.

In times of serious unrest, such as occurred after the Sharpeville massacre in March 1960, or in 1985, the government can introduce a State of Emergency. Anyone whom the government regards as a threat can be held in detention for as long as the Emergency lasts. At the moment many children, some as young as 12, have been in detention for many months. They are not allowed to see a lawyer or their parents. Many of the detainees are also ill-treated and beaten up during questioning. Since 1963, 69 people have died in detention.

The South African government uses other measures to silence opposition. Censorship is widespread and books, newspapers and films are banned. Another measure is to issue a Banning Order against a named person. Someone who is banned is not charged in court with any offence. It is simply an order from the Minister of Justice. A banned person cannot move from his home area, cannot meet with more than three people at one time and cannot be referred to in newspapers or on television.

Any police officer has the right to ask for a black's passbook. While the government claim that the Passbook Laws are to be repealed, all South Africans will still have to carry an identity document.

SOURCE 79 — How the Terrorism Act works

Any person who commits any act likely to encourage feelings of hostility between the white and other inhabitants of South Africa is guilty of a criminal offence under the terms of the Terrorism Act which is punishable by the death penalty.
('Apartheid in Practice', UN Publications, 1976.)

SOURCE 80 — A Government Minister justifies detention

You won't get much information from a detainee if you keep him in a five star hotel with a friend.

If a limited period of detention were laid down terrorists would be prepared in advance to withstand questioning for that period.
(Louis Le Grange, Minister of Law and Order.)

SOURCE 81 — What is an Act of Terrorism?

A young black man wrote a violently anti-white poem. By sending it to a seventeen-year-old girl he was deemed to have published it. He was sentenced to the minimum of five years' imprisonment with no parole or remission.
('The White Tribe of Africa', by David Harrison, BBC Publications, 1981.)

SOURCE 82 — The treatment of detainees

After the 1985 State of Emergency researchers from the University of Cape Town interviewed a sample of 176 detainees. They found that:
83 per cent claimed some form of physical abuse.
75 per cent reported being beaten.
25 per cent said they had been subjected to electric shocks.
18 per cent said they had been subjected to strangulation.
80 per cent claimed to have been held in solitary confinement.
('The Apartheid Handbook', by Roger Omond, Penguin Books, 1986.)

◀ Using all the Sources, can you explain why it is difficult to protest against the system of apartheid in South Africa?

◀ What can happen to opponents of the government in South Africa?

The Death of Bantu Steve Biko

Steve Biko was the leader of the Black People's Consciousness Movement in the 1970s. He had been arrested on previous occasions because of his opposition to apartheid. He was also a banned person and was arrested in August 1977 for breaking his Banning Order. He was taken to Port Elizabeth police station in the Eastern Cape and held for questioning for three weeks. He was placed unconscious on the floor of a Land-Rover and driven 700 miles to Pretoria and died shortly after.

The Minister of Justice, James Kruger, announced that Steve Biko had died after a hunger strike. It soon became clear that he had been injured in detention and died of head injuries. At the inquest Sidney Kentridge, the lawyer for the Biko family, tried to prove that he had been deliberately injured by members of the Security Police.

SOURCE 83 — The cause of death
The Chief State Pathologist's report stated that Steve Biko died of extensive head injuries and kidney failure. The report also mentioned abrasions to the left forehead, injuries to the chest and other numerous but minor injuries.

SOURCE 84 — Major Snyman describes how Steve Biko was injured
Shortly after Mr Biko had his handcuffs and leg irons removed he got a wild expression in his eyes and jumped off the chair. Major Snyman and Captain Siebert tried to grab Mr Biko who was clearly beside himself with fury. In the process they knocked against the tables in the office. The struggle lasted several minutes.

SOURCE 85 — Major Snyman denies assaulting Steve Biko
Mr Kentridge asked Major Snyman if he made threats to Mr Biko. Major Snyman denied making threats or putting pressure on Mr Biko. He had unlimited time to get the information and it would not have paid the police to assault Mr Biko for information.

SOURCE 86 — The findings of the Autopsy
Mr Kentridge said, summing up Professor Proctor's evidence, that there were five distinct lesions (a change in the appearance of an organ due to injury) in Mr Biko's brain and that the infliction of those lesions would have required at least three or four blows to the head. The first and probably fatal lesions on the side of the brain were probably caused by a blow to the other side of the head. He said that Mr Biko had suffered moderate to severe brain injury. In the case of a moderate injury he estimated that ten to twenty minutes of unconsciousness was reasonable.

SOURCE 87 — Professor Loubser's evidence
Professor Loubser said that the scab that appeared on the surface of Mr Biko's head was the one aspect of his injuries compatible with a blow from a truncheon. Professor Loubser agreed that the cuts on the lip were more likely to have been caused by two blows than a fall.

Steve Biko, one of the founders and leaders of the Black Consciousness Movement. His qualities of leadership soon brought him to the attention of the authorities. He had been arrested and detained numerous times and was under a banning order when arrested in 1977. He died in detention; the government first claimed that his death was the result of a hunger strike.

49

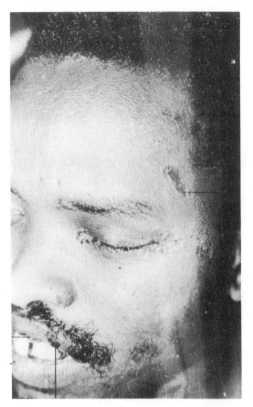

Steve Biko, showing the injuries to his head and face.

SOURCE 88 — The consequences of Steve Biko's head injuries

Mr Kentridge said that the medical experts advising him had expressed the view that Mr Biko's injury must have been followed by a period of unconsciousness of at least ten minutes. The police account of the struggle did not mention a period of unconsciousness; in that case the injuries could not have been sustained during the struggle. What he found difficult to believe was that a conscious man falling to the ground could sustain such an injury.

SOURCE 89 — Mr Kentridge sums up the evidence

The submission was that one or more members of the Security Police had been responsible for Mr Biko's death and that the injury had been inflicted deliberately or negligently. Mr Biko had been beaten and the person or persons who did this had not at the time cared whether serious injury had resulted or not.

SOURCE 90 — Mr van Rooyen sums up the evidence for the police

The court faced two possibilities — that the injury was self-inflicted or that the injury was sustained during the struggle on the morning of 7 September. Various witnesses had testified to this. The court could accept as fact that there had been a violent episode and that this was started by Mr Biko. As far as the Security Police were concerned the court would not be able to find that they were involved in any act which led to Mr Biko's death.

SOURCE 91 — The findings of the inquest

1. That Stephen Biko died on 12 September 1977 and that the cause of death was brain injury which led to kidney failure and other complications.
2. That the head injuries were probably sustained on 7 September in a scuffle in the Security Police Headquarters in Port Elizabeth.
3. That on the available evidence the death could not be blamed on any act or omission amounting to a criminal offence on the part of any person.

Questions

1. From Sources 83 and 86, what caused the death of Steve Biko?
2. What would have been the immediate result of the injuries which were described in Source 88?
3. Is there anything in Sources 86 and 88 which is not confirmed in Source 84?
4. How does Major Snyman allege that the injuries took place?
5. Is this confirmed in Sources 86, 87 and 88?
6. Why do you think that the police tried to prove that Steve Biko sustained his injuries as described in Source 84?

7. What is the case that Sidney Kentridge is trying to prove? How does this differ from the case put forward by the police?
8. Are the findings of the inquest in line with the evidence presented? Are there any criticisms you could make of the conclusions?
9. Using all the available evidence, what do you think caused Steve Biko's death?

Architects of Apartheid

Daniel Malan, founder of the National Party and leader of the government which introduced apartheid in 1948.

This chapter deals with the following topics:
The careers of Daniel Malan and Hendrik Verwoerd.

After reading this chapter and completing the exercises you will have:
Examined the part played by Daniel Malan and Hendrik Verwoerd in the development of apartheid in South Africa.

Daniel Malan and Hendrik Verwoerd played crucial roles in the development of Afrikaner Nationalism. While Malan led the government that introduced apartheid, his most important contribution to Nationalist politics came in the years before 1948. Verwoerd, on the other hand, refined the idea of apartheid and gave it a new direction in the 1960s. The South Africa of today is very much the creation of Verwoerd.

Daniel Malan was a Minister in the Dutch Reformed Church who first made a name for himself as editor of *De Burger,* a Nationalist newspaper. He entered Parliament in 1919 and became a minister in Hertzog's government in 1924. In 1934 he resigned from Hertzog's National Party in protest at the amalgamation with Smuts's South Africa Party. He formed his own 'Purified' National Party. Many thought that Malan's influence would fade, but with the outbreak of the Second World War the 'Purified' National Party spoke for most Afrikaner Nationalists.

Smuts claimed that the victory of the National Party in the 1948 election was simply a desire for change. For Malan it was the beginning of a new age in South Africa. Malan's policies were to put the Afrikaner firmly in control. The South African government has been in the hands of the National Party since 1948.

SOURCE 92 — The 'Purified' National Party
The original Trekkers wanted freedom to preserve themselves as a White Race. Their task to make South Africa a white man's land is ten times more your task today. Have you the patriotism in this year of celebration to use this God-given opportunity to demand that White Civilisation will be assured?
(Daniel Malan, speaking in 1938 during the centenary celebrations of the Great Trek.)

The following are extracts from the Constitution of the National Party which was drawn up in 1941. It shows the kind of South Africa that Nationalists wanted. Malan played an important part in drafting the document.

SOURCE 93 — The Proposed Constitution of the National Party
Afrikaans, as the language of the original white inhabitants of the country, will be the first official language, English will be regarded as a second or supplementary official language.

Every coloured group of races will be segregated, not only as regards the place of dwelling but also with regard to the type of work. The members of such groups can be allowed to enter white territories under proper lawful control for work.

The mixing of blood between whites and non-whites is forbidden.

The existence of any political organisation which is in strife with the Christian and national principles of the state is forbidden.
('The Rise of the South African Reich' by Brian Bunting, IDAF Publications, 1986.)

SOURCE 94 — The Nationalist election victory 1948
Today South Africa belongs to us once more. For the first time since the Union South Africa is our own. May God grant that it will always remain so.
(Malan's reaction to his election victory.)

The Architects of Apartheid: The Role of Individuals

Hendrik Verwoerd

Hendrik Verwoerd, Prime Minister from 1959 to 1966. The Homelands policy was his idea.

Verwoerd was born in the Netherlands, but moved to South Africa as a young child in 1903. At the University of Stellenbosch he became a convinced Afrikaner Nationalist and was a member of the Broederbond before he was 30. In 1937 he became editor of *Die Transvaaler,* a Nationalist newspaper, and through the paper he expressed admiration for the Nazis and was opposed to Jewish immigration to South Africa.

Verwoerd became Vice-Chairman of the Transvaal National Party in 1946 and entered Parliament in 1950. Recognising his talent, Malan soon made him Minister of Native Affairs. Verwoerd was responsible for shaping and putting into effect many aspects of the policy of apartheid. He tried to sell the policy to the world in quite harmless terms. He described apartheid as a policy of 'good neighbourliness'. This contrasted with his views on the position of the African in white South Africa. Verwoerd's most important creation was the idea of 'Grand Apartheid' — setting up independent black nations which have become known as Homelands. Verwoerd was assassinated in 1966 by a white man who worked in the South African Parliament.

SOURCE 95 — Verwoerd on the Role of Africans in South Africa
Schools must equip the Bantu to meet the demands which life in South Africa will impose on him. There is no place for him in the European community above the level of certain forms of labour. What is the use of teaching a Bantu child mathematics when he cannot use it in practice. Until now education drew him away from his own community by showing him the green pastures of European society in which he is not allowed to graze.
(Hendrik Verwoerd speaking in 1953 about the Bantu Education Act.)

SOURCE 96 — The Homelands Policy
While the white man would remain the ruler of white South Africa, the white man as the guardian of the black man will see to it that his development does take place; in such a fashion that the black masses as they become free really do become free. We will not force independence on them from outside or from above. We will build up their democratic freedom from the bottom upwards so that as freedom is obtained the masses will be right for it.
(Hendrik Verwoerd outlining his plans for independent homelands.)

SOURCE 97 — Other opinions of Verwoerd

He saw himself as the Messiah, he knew all the answers, he laid down the law, he told you what to do. Yours was not to question or to query just get on with the job. I had a written instruction from Verwoerd that in no circumstances was I to shake hands with a black man when he came to see me in my office. There was no familiarity, no friendliness. When writing to a black man I was instructed not to use the normal form of address: 'Dear Sir' but simply an African word which meant 'Man'.

(William Carr, Director of African Affairs in Johannesburg.)

Verwoerd did not just distinguish between white and black, it was white — non-white. This is basically racism. If you look at everything that he applied it was racism. All the lifts in public buildings in South Africa were segregated, the public counters in Post Offices white and non-white, even a non-white taxi couldn't carry the luggage of a white man.

(South African Race Relations Expert.)

Questions

1. In what ways was Daniel Malan an Afrikaner Nationalist?
2. Using Sources 92 and 93, how did Malan contribute to the success of the National Party in the years before 1948?
3. What do you think Malan meant by his statement in Source 94?
4. From what you have read in previous chapters, which clauses of the 1941 constitution eventually became law after 1948? Can you identify the actual laws?

5. What contribution did Verwoerd make to the development of apartheid after 1948?
6. Verwoerd publicly described apartheid as a policy of 'good neighbourliness'. From reading Sources 95, 96 and 97 do you think he really had the interests of the Africans at heart?

Living with Apartheid

This chapter deals with the following topic:
How apartheid affects the everyday life of non-white South Africans.

After reading this chapter and completing the exercises you will have:
1. Looked at life in South Africa from the viewpoint of those most directly affected.
2. Examined and interpreted a wide variety of statistical information and used it to understand some of the disadvantages faced by non-white South Africans.

Apartheid is much more than signs which say 'Europeans Only' or 'Non-Whites'. It is a policy which reaches all through South African society. It affects housing, employment, education, health, pensions and social security benefits. Even death is unequal in South Africa. In this chapter black South Africans explain how their lives are affected by apartheid. Statistics may just be figures on paper or graphs but they, too, have an important part to play in showing just how unequal South African society is. The first extracts show how 'Petty Apartheid' and the Separate Amenities Act affected people's lives. This was the aspect of apartheid that was most visible and that reminded non-whites every day of their position in South Africa.

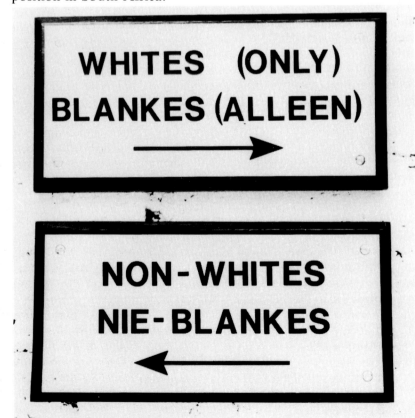

The Separate Amenities Law was responsible for introducing many of the most annoying features of apartheid. Signs like this one were a common feature of life in South Africa and were a constant reminder to all South Africans that they were living in an unequal society. While the Act has been repealed and many facilities are now integrated, local authorities and private businesses can still discriminate in this way. Beaches, swimming pools and washrooms are still segregated in many parts of South Africa.

54

SOURCE 98 — Winnie Mandela goes shopping

I remember an instance in the only fashion shop in Brandfort. Just imagine how blacks were being served there: they must stand in the door and point out to the white owner 'Can I see that dress?' and the owner takes it from the rail and brings it to the door. It was unthinkable that a black woman would come inside and touch a dress that a white woman would touch after her. These small things are so humiliating, an insult to one's dignity.

One day I went to the dress shop. The white saleswoman was standing in the doorway and as I thought she wanted to go outside I pushed her aside and went in. She came after us and told us to get outside. I said no we want to look at a dress. She said that we had to stand outside. There was such a furious exchange. By the time we left there must have been a hundred people outside. Finally the police were called.

(Winnie Mandela, 'Part of My Soul', Penguin Books, 1985.)

Verwoerd said that there was no point in teaching African children mathematics.

SOURCE 99 — African Education

The education system in Soweto has been planned by the nationalist regime to retard the progress of African people in general. It is designed to humiliate and discourage them. To make the Blacks a subservient workforce.

Academic performance is poor because of the shortage of teachers and overcrowding. The double session known as the 'hot system' was introduced by the Bantu Education Department to increase the number of children who could be admitted into existing primary schools. Also pupils start school in Soweto at the age of seven compared to five for white children.

To ensure that a limited number of children enrol in Soweto schools the government has introduced a pink card for each pupil. The card states that a pupil's name is on a registered house permit. Those children whose names do not appear on a house permit do not get pink cards and can't go to school.

('Window on Soweto', Joyce Sikakane, IDAF Publications, 1976.)

SOURCE 100 — The effects of 'Bantu Education'

Bantu Education produces young blacks who suffer from lack of confidence in dealing with privileged whites and whose skill in communication and understanding is poorly developed. Their command of English, even as a second language is unsatisfactory.

(Comment made by the Headmaster of a White private school in Johannesburg.)

Overcrowding and inferior facilities place African children at a disadvantage.

Living with Apartheid — life for non-Whites in South Africa

Housing in Soweto.

SOURCE 101 — Living in Soweto

Soweto (called So-where-to by the people who live there) is the largest single ghetto in Africa. Its name is taken from its location SOuth WEst TOwnships. It covers 85 square kilometres. 108,766 red or grey brick houses are built opposite each other in straight rows. Most homes use candles, paraffin or gas lamps for lighting. Coal stoves are used in almost all the homes. Only a quarter of the houses in Soweto have running cold water inside the house. The majority have outside taps. Only three houses in a hundred have hot water, only seven in a hundred have a bath or a shower.
('Window on Soweto', Joyce Sikakane, IDAF Publications, 1976.)

Many workers do not have the right to live in townships. They may have to travel long distances every day from the Homelands to Johannesburg or Pretoria. Many miners from the Homelands live too far away to commute. They have to live in migrant hostels and only return to see their families once or twice a year.

A study of commuters between one of the Homelands and Pretoria found that:

SOURCE 102 — Commuting

Most commuters, who travel between 70 and 80 miles by bus to work in Pretoria, left home before 5 a.m. and spent two to three hours on a bus each day. More than half were away from home for more than 14 hours a day.

A quarter spent three hours or more on a bus each day.

At the time of the survey 17.5 per cent of the weekly average wage was spent on bus fares.
('The Apartheid Handbook', Roger Omond, Penguin Books, 1986.)

◀ How do the following affect the everyday life of Africans living in South Africa:
1. The Separate Amenities Acts?
2. The Bantu Education Act?
3. The Group Areas Act?

Soweto from the air. A huge sprawling black city with few facilities. There are few opportunities for work in Soweto and most Africans have to commute to Johannesburg every day. The planning shows a lack of imagination and the aim was to get as many houses as possible into an area.

SOURCE 103 — Migrant Hostels

In Soweto 60,000 men are hostel dwellers. Barbed wire fences divide the hostels from the rest of the townships. There are no dining rooms, no visitors rooms, no recreation facilities and absolutely no privacy for the inmates. Women are not allowed into the hostels. The occupants are respectable married men forced to leave their wives and children. There are also divorced men and single men. By law no single man is allowed to rent a house in Soweto.

('Window on Soweto', Joyce Sikakane, IDAF Publications, 1976.)

SOURCE 104 — The Commonwealth Eminent Persons Group

Blacks do not have equal access to jobs; despite the recent abolition of job reservation laws, inadequate education and training maintains white dominance in clerical jobs. Further, blacks are paid much less than whites for the same jobs. Average black earnings are less than a quarter of white earnings. Blacks are also more likely to be unemployed. Some estimates put black unemployment at more than 3 million in a labour force of 7 to 9 million.

('Mission to South Africa', The Commonwealth Eminent Persons Group on South Africa, Penguin Books, 1986.)

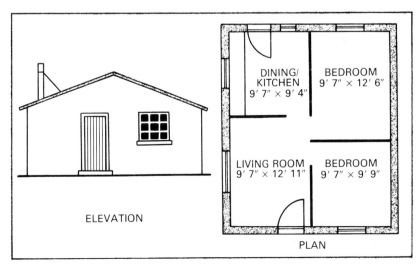

Accommodation is cramped and until recently there were very few houses with electricity and even fewer with bathrooms or hot and cold running water.

The next pages present statistical information that illustrates how apartheid affects many aspects of life in South Africa.

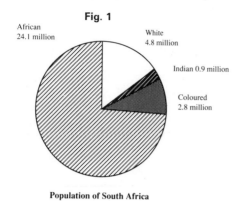

Fig. 1

Population of South Africa

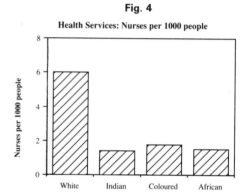

Fig. 2

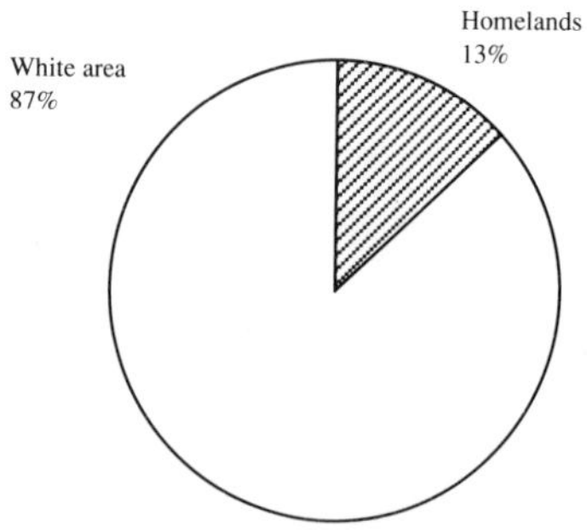

Land distribution

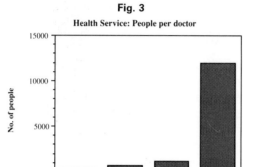

Fig. 3

Health Service: People per doctor

Fig. 4

Health Services: Nurses per 1000 people

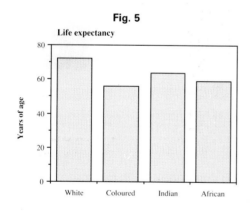

Fig. 5

Life expectancy

Fig. 6

Infant Mortality Rates

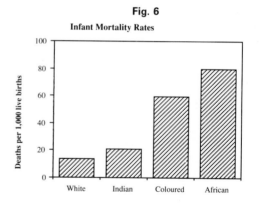

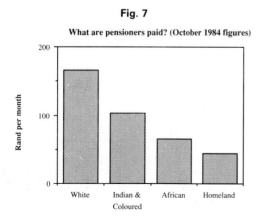

Fig. 7

What are pensioners paid? (October 1984 figures)

Fig. 8

Percentage of pension budget

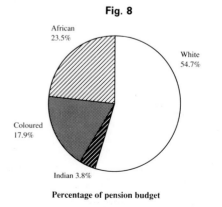

Fig. 9
Housing Shortages

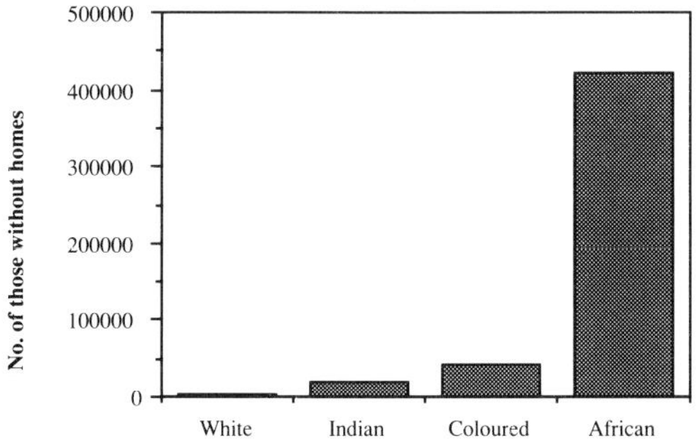

Fig. 10
Spending on child welfare

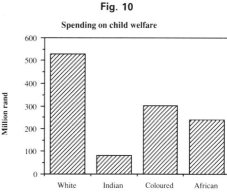

Fig. 11
Average income per month in 1984

Fig. 12
Occupation: Labouring jobs

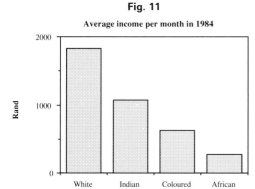

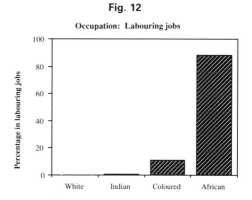

Fig. 13
Occupation: Service jobs

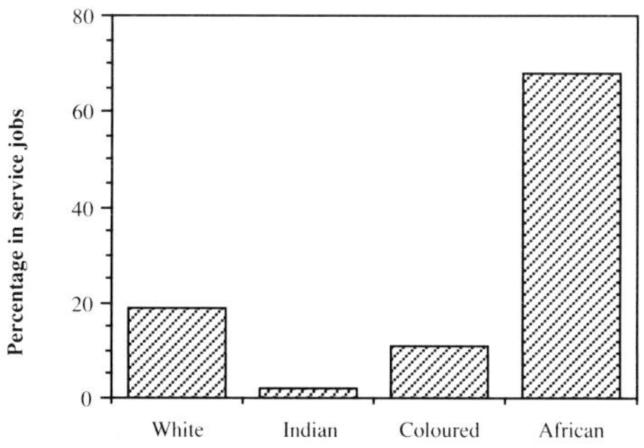

Fig. 14
Occupation: Managerial posts

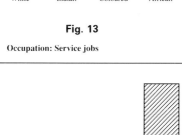

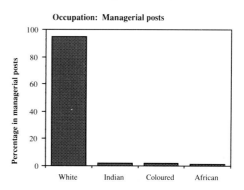

Questions

1. From Figs. 1 and 2 what conclusions can you draw between the size of the different population groups and land distribution?
2. What do the statistics in Figs. 3, 4, 5 and 6 reveal about health care for the different groups in South Africa?
3. Is the statement by the Eminent Persons Group in Source 104 backed up by the statistical evidence in Figs. 3-14?

The African National Congress

This chapter deals with the following topics:
1. The Founding of the ANC.
2. Why the ANC was created.
3. The ideas of the ANC.
4. The ANC today.

After reading this chapter and completing the exercises you will have:
1. Examined the factors responsible for the formation of the ANC.
2. The main ideas of the ANC.
3. The influence of the ideas of the ANC in South Africa and in the rest of Africa.

The creation of the Union of South Africa was meant to heal the wounds of the Boer War. In doing so the interests of the Africans were overlooked. Africans in the Cape had been given the right to vote in 1860. After the formation of the Union these rights were not to be extended to the rest of South Africa. One of the first laws passed by the new Union was the Mines and Works Act which limited the type of work which Africans could do. In 1912 educated and middle class Africans met in Bloemfontein to unite to defend the interests of all Africans. The South Africa Natives National Congress was the forerunner of the African National Congress. The leading light in the formation of the SANNC was a young lawyer Pixley Seme. Seme wanted a party which would unite all Africans and ignore traditional tribal divisions.

SOURCE 105 — The founding of the South African Natives National Congress
Chiefs of royal blood and gentlemen of our race . . . we have discovered that in the land of our birth, Africans are treated as hewers of wood and drawers of water. The whites of this country have formed the Union of South Africa, a Union in which we have no voice in the making of laws and no part in the government. We have asked you therefore, to this conference so that together we can find ways of creating national unity and defending our rights and privileges.
('Nelson Mandela', by Mary Benson, Penguin Books, 1986.)

Pixley Ka Seme, one of the founders of the South African Natives National Congress which eventually became the ANC. Seme was alarmed by the way that African interests were ignored when the Union of South Africa was established. He saw that the SANNC could be an effective voice for unifying African protest. One of the ideas of the SANNC was that it was for all Africans regardless of tribal origin.

The SANNC members were mostly from the small African middle class: lawyers, teachers and other white-collar occupations. They hoped to end the colour bar by petitions and lobbying. Delegations were sent to London and the Peace Conference at Paris after the First World War. Their influence was small and they were easily ignored. In the 1920s the most active organisation fighting for African rights was the Industrial and Commercial Workers Union; at the height of its popularity it had over 250,000 members.

SOURCE 106 — The ANC in the Inter-War years
The Congress placed importance on political campaigning while the ICU staged some important strikes but faced fresh laws to prevent real industrial organisation and put a stop to public meetings in black areas. The ANC was troubled by internal problems. During the depression years these disputes so severely weakened Congress that some described the ANC as moribund (dying) in this period.
('Spear of the Nation', International Broadcasting Trust, 1986.)

It was not until the Second World War that the fortunes of the ANC revived. This was largely due to new younger members joining — men such as Oliver Tambo, Walter Sisulu, Anton Lembede and Nelson Mandela. Together they formed the Youth Wing of the ANC. These men and the ideas of the Youth League were to change the ANC from a mainly middle-class group with limited support to a popular party supported by all Africans.

The ANC: The Influence of a New Group

While the Youth Wing were injecting new life into the ANC, its leader, Dr A B Xuma, was making links with other organisations in South Africa. He wanted to create an alliance of groups who had a common interest in opposing the policies of the white government. Xuma persuaded the South African Communist Party and the South African Indian Congress, led by Manilal Gandhi, to join in protests against the Pass Laws. The campaign was not a success, but the contacts with other groups were to be very important.

SOURCE 107 — The Youth League Manifesto 1944
The aim of our struggle is Africanism and our motto is 'Africa's Cause Must Triumph'.

We believe that the national liberation of Africans will be achieved by Africans themselves. We reject foreign leadership of Africa. We may borrow useful ideologies* but we reject the wholesale importing of foreign ideologies into Africa.

We believe in the unity of all Africans from the Mediterranean Sea in the North to the Indian and Atlantic Oceans in the South. We believe that Africans must speak with one voice.
('Nelson Mandela: The Struggle is my Life', IDAF Publications, 1986.)
* Ideologies: A set of political ideas or beliefs.

SOURCE 108 — The Programme of Action 1949
The principles of the Programme of Action of the African National Congress are inspired by the desire to achieve national freedom. This implies the rejection of segregation, apartheid and domination of the white over blacks.

We will appoint a council of action whose function should be to carry into effect the programme which shall:
Undertake a campaign to educate our people.
Employ the following weapons: immediate boycott, strikes, civil disobedience, non-co-operation.
Preparations and making of plans for a national stoppage for one day as a mark of protest against the policy of the government.

SOURCE 109 — The Aims of the ANC in the 1980s

When we say we are fighting for a united democratic and non-racial South Africa, we mean what we say. It is very clear to us that unless our country becomes such an entity, we shall know no peace. As long as the apartheid system exists a terrible collision between ourselves and our opponents is inevitable. Many battles will be fought and many lives will be lost throughout our region. Yet the outcome is not in doubt. Our people have decided that our country must advance as rapidly as possible to the situation where they, black and white will govern themselves as equals. Whatever the cost there is no doubt that we will win.

(Part of the Canon Collins Memorial Lecture given by Oliver Tambo, President of the ANC in May 1987.)

SOURCE 110 — An independent assessment of the ANC

There can be no negotiated settlement in South Africa without the ANC; the breadth of its support is undeniable and this support is growing. The open identification with the ANC through banners and songs, in funerals and in churches throughout the country, supports the widely held belief that if an election were held today the ANC would win.

('Mission to South Africa', the Findings of the Commonwealth Eminent Persons Group, Penguin Books, 1986.)

Questions

1. What reasons did Pixley ka Seme give for forming the SANCC?
2. From Sources 105 and 106 how effective was the ANC in the first years of its existence?
3. What does Source 107 reveal about the views of the ANC Youth Wing on:
   a. Nationalism?
   b. Communism?
4. From Sources 107 and 108 what policies of the ANC are:
   a. the same
   b. different
   from those outlined in Source 109.
5. Today the ANC is a banned organisation; its leaders are either in exile or in prison. Despite this, how important is the ANC in the 1980s?

Architects of Resistance

This chapter deals with the following topic:
1. The careers of Albert Luthuli and Nelson Mandela.

After reading this chapter and completing the exercises you will have:
1. Examined the part played by Albert Luthuli and Nelson Mandela in the development of the ANC.
2. Understood the important part played by these men in the struggle for civil rights.

In the 1950s and 1960s Albert Luthuli and Nelson Mandela were well known outside South Africa as leaders of the fight against apartheid. Albert Luthuli was descended from the Zulu chiefs of Natal. He was brought up in a Christian missionary village and for a while trained to be a teacher. In 1936 he was elected a chief of his village and later became a member of the Natives Representation Council, (NRC), but it was a job that did not last long. In 1946 he was travelling to Pretoria to a meeting of the NRC. Along with other African members of the NRC, Luthuli witnessed the brutal way the police dealt with striking African miners. The government refused to hold an inquiry into the miners' complaints. As a result, Luthuli spoke out against the government at the meeting of the NRC and was later dismissed from the Council.

It was natural that an outspoken man like Luthuli became involved with the ANC. 'I am in Congress because I am a Christian,' he told anyone who asked. Luthuli's sense of justice and his dislike of apartheid was based on his strong Christian principles. When visiting America and Europe it was obvious to all who met him that Albert Luthuli was not a dangerous revolutionary. Out of South Africa he was able to put forward the views of the ANC without worrying about banning orders. Above all, he was treated with respect, which contrasted with the way he was dealt with in South Africa.

His arrest on charges of treason in 1956 shocked many. In 1960 he was awarded the Nobel Peace Prize, but this did not prevent further arrests and Banning Orders. This rebounded on the authorities. The more the government tried to silence Luthuli, the better known he became in the outside world.

Albert Luthuli, Zulu chief and member of the Natives Representation Council. He spoke out against the ineffectiveness of the NRC and was eventually sacked. He became the leader of the ANC. He was a popular and unifying figure who was well-known and respected outside South Africa.

SOURCE 111 — Luthuli's speech to the NRC

I remember saying that the house was on fire and I would add fuel to the fire. Being newly elected to the Natives Representation Council I was in a good position to assess the disillusioned mood of the people:

Disillusioned because the Council was ignored.
Disillusioned because the Council seemed irrelevant.
Disillusioned because in ten years the council had done nothing.

Chapter 13

The council had approached the government with request after request, only to be ignored.

When I sat down it was obvious that the white official in the chair was much upset by what I had said and he was not able to disguise it. He had expected something milder from a newly elected chief.
('Let My People Go', by Albert Luthuli, Fontana, 1962.)

SOURCE 112 — Chief Luthuli and the Nobel Peace Prize

After receiving the Peace Prize Chief Luthuli said that award recognised the part played by himself and many others in the ANC who had tried for 50 years to find a peaceful solution to the problems of South Africa. He said he was grateful for the support given to his peoples' struggle by progressive governments throughout the world. People were recognising the part played by Africans for political freedom and a desire for a world where people were judged on merit and not race.

Even after the Sharpeville Massacre and the banning of the ANC, Luthuli remained committed to non-violence. He was not involved in the founding of the Umkhonto We Sizwe, but understood the motives of Nelson Mandela and the others who formed Umkhonto.

Nelson Mandela came from a similar royal background to Albert Luthuli's. His interest in politics started while he was a student at Fort Hare University in the Eastern Cape. During the Second World War Mandela moved to Johannesburg where he met Walter Sisulu. Sisulu was an important influence and introduced him to the ANC. Mandela became a leading member of the Youth Wing of the ANC. As a member of the Youth Wing he was opposed to the influence of the Communist Party in the Congress and rejected help from white South Africans. It was as a lawyer that Mandela came face-to-face with the way that Africans were treated in their own country.

Nelson Mandela's legal background made him an important figure in the ANC. He was a capable organiser and natural leader. After Sharpeville in 1960 he realised that non-violent protest had its limits and was involved in the creation of the military wing of the ANC. Despite being imprisoned since 1963, he is regarded by many Africans as their leader.

SOURCE 113 — Nelson Mandela the lawyer

South Africa has the dubious reputation of boasting one of the highest prison populations in the world. Jails are jam packed with people. To cheek a white man can be a crime, to live in the wrong area can be a crime. South African laws turn innocent people into criminals.

The living conditions of the people are unbearable. The cost of milk, meat and vegetables is beyond the pockets of an average family. Because of the lack of proper medical facilities our people are ravaged by T.B., leprosy and infant mortality.
('Nelson Mandela: The Struggle Is My Life', IDAF Publications, 1986.)

Nelson Mandela's real influence was as an organiser. Nelson Mandela is a powerful personality and has a natural charm. He makes a great impression on all who meet him. Together with other members of the Youth League: Walter Sisulu, Anton Lembede and Oliver Tambo, they gave new life to the ANC in the years after the Second World War. The Programme of Action was a complete change of tactics. After 1949 the ANC was to use non-violent direct action to try to bring about change.

In the years following 1949 there was a series of court appearances and banning orders, including the four-year treason trial. When this ended in 1961 Nelson Mandela went underground. The security police tried to catch him without success. He was known romantically as the 'Black Pimpernel'. While on the run, Mandela became convinced that new methods were needed. The non-violent protests had not ended apartheid. Mandela was involved in the creation of Umkhonto We Sizwe, which started a campaign of sabotage. In October 1963 the leaders of Umkhonto were put on trial for High Treason and sentenced to life imprisonment.

SOURCE 114 — Nelson Mandela rejects President Botha's offer of freedom in 1985

I cherish my own freedom dearly, but I care even more for your freedom. Too many have died since I went to prison. Too many have suffered for the love of freedom. I owe it to their widows, to their orphans, to their mothers and their fathers who have wept for them.

Not only have I suffered during these long lonely wasted years. I am no less life loving than you are, but I cannot sell the birthright of the people to be free.

Only free men can negotiate. Prisoners cannot enter into contracts. Your freedom and mine cannot be separated.

To this day Nelson Mandela remains in prison, but he is not a forgotten man. His influence in South Africa is if anything stronger. Demands for his release come from all over the world. In South Africa he is a banned person and it is against the law to display his photograph or quote from his speeches. The South African government realises that Nelson Mandela is looked to as a leader by many black South Africans. He was offered his freedom by the government in 1985 on the condition that he rejected violence as a political weapon.

SOURCE 115 — An assessment of Nelson Mandela's importance

Nelson Mandela impressed us as an outstandingly able and sincere person whose qualities of leadership were self evident. We found him unmarked by any trace of bitterness despite his long imprisonment. His overriding concern was for the welfare of all races in South Africa in a just society. According to all the evidence Nelson Mandela is a unifying, commanding and popular leader. Recent opinion polls revealed that blacks, Indians and coloureds look to Nelson Mandela as the leader of a non-racial South Africa.
('Mission to South Africa', the Report of the Commonwealth Eminent Persons Group on South Africa, Penguin Books, 1986.)

Questions
1. How important was Christianity to Albert Luthuli?
2. After reading Source 111 can you suggest why Luthuli was sacked as a member of the Natives Representation Council?
3. From Sources 111 and 112 can you explain why:
   a. Albert Luthuli was an important figure in the ANC.
   b. He was well known in the outside world?
4. As a successful solicitor in Johannesburg how was Nelson Mandela able to witness first-hand the conditions he describes in Source 113?
5. If Nelson Mandela has been in prison since 1963 can he still be an influential figure in South Africa? Can you explain this fact?

Freedom Charter and Treason Trial

This chapter deals with the following topics:
1. The background to the Freedom Charter.
2. The Freedom Charter.
3. The effect of the Freedom Charter in South Africa.
4. The Treason Trial.

After reading this chapter and completing the exercises you will have:
1. Looked at the events that shaped the Freedom Charter.
2. Seen that the Freedom Charter marked a new stage in the opposition to apartheid.
3. Discovered that the Treason Trial was a consequence of the Freedom Charter.

After the election of the Nationalist government in 1948 the ANC realised that the struggle for black rights was entering a new phase. Under pressure from the Youth Wing, a new Programme of Action was adopted that was to use different methods. Albert Luthuli said it was time to replace words with action. The Defiance Campaign of 1952 planned large-scale illegal marches and demonstrations. Protestors would allow themselves to be arrested. The slogan of the Campaign was: 'Hey Malan! Open the jail doors we want to enter.' The leaders of the ANC were arrested, some imprisoned and others banned. The government did not alter a single law, but the membership of the ANC leapt from 7000 to over 100,000.

The next stage of the campaign was the Congress of the People. This was the idea of Professor Z. K. Matthews, a former leader of the ANC. The aim was to unite all groups in South Africa who were opposed to apartheid and put forward their ideas for a free and equal South Africa. The Congress Alliance included the ANC, the Indian National Congress, the South African Congress of Trade Unions and many church groups. Members of the Congress Alliance toured South Africa asking people for their ideas on the future of South Africa.

SOURCE 116 — Congress Alliance publicity

IF YOU COULD MAKE THE LAWS WHAT WOULD YOU DO?

HOW WOULD YOU MAKE SOUTH AFRICA A HAPPY PLACE FOR ALL THE PEOPLE?

Let us speak of the wide lands and the narrow strips on which we toil.

Let us speak of brothers without land and the children without schooling.

Let us speak of taxes and of cattle and of famine.

LET US SPEAK OF FREEDOM!

We call on the miners of coal, gold and diamonds. Let us speak of the dark shafts and the cold compounds far from our families.
('Nelson Mandela: The Struggle is My Life', IDAF Publications, 1986.)

Delegates arrive for the Congress of the People in Kliptown in 1955. The placards show some of the reforms which became part of the Freedom Charter.

SOURCE 117 — The Congress of the People

Thousands turned up from all over South Africa, in spite of police attempts to stop them arriving. Buses were held up and railway carriages carrying delegates to Kliptown were mysteriously uncoupled and left in sidings. There were thousands there all in a holiday mood; it looked just like Derby Day, it was a marvellous weekend.

The main work of the Congress was to pass what has become known as the Freedom Charter and clause by clause this Freedom Charter spelt out what kind of South Africa people really wanted to live in.

(Bishop Trevor Huddlestone describing the Congress of the People held at Kliptown near Johannesburg in June 1955.)

The Freedom Charter: A Turning Point in Black Opposition

The Freedom Charter has been compared to the American Declaration of Independence; it outlined for the first time the ideas of those South Africans opposed to the Nationalist government. The Charter has remained a series of political demands and the ANC still believe that the ideas in the Freedom Charter are the foundation for a free and equal South Africa. The simple style of the Charter means that it can be understood by everyone. The Commonwealth Eminent Persons Group which visited South Africa in 1985 described the People's Congress as 'the most representative gathering ever held in South Africa.'

SOURCE 118 — The Freedom Charter
WE, THE PEOPLE OF SOUTH AFRICA, DECLARE FOR ALL OUR COUNTRY AND THE WORLD TO KNOW:

That South Africa belongs to all who live in it. That our people have been robbed of their birthright to land, liberty and peace.

That only a democratic state based on the will of all the people, can secure to all their birthright without distinction of colour, race, sex or belief.

Below are some of the important sections of the Charter:

THE PEOPLE SHALL GOVERN.
ALL NATIONAL GROUPS SHALL HAVE EQUAL RIGHTS.
ALL SHALL BE EQUAL BEFORE THE LAW.
ALL SHALL ENJOY EQUAL HUMAN RIGHTS.
THERE SHALL BE PEACE AND FRIENDSHIP.

Let all those who love their people and the country now say, as we say here:

'These freedoms we will fight for, side by side, throughout our lives, until we have won liberty.'

SOURCE 119 — Chief Luthuli and the importance of the Freedom Charter
The Congress of the People had far-reaching effects. Nothing in the history of South Africa quite caught the popular imagination. Even remote rural areas were aware of what was going on. The noisy opposition of the white press advertised the Congress and the Freedom Charter more effectively than our own efforts would have done. 'If the white press object on this scale', most Africans felt, 'it must be a good thing.'
('Let My People Go', by Albert Luthuli, Fontana, 1962.)

SOURCE 120 — The Government response to the Congress and the Charter
Being the product of a broad alliance of South Africa representing almost every political shade, the Freedom Charter had to include democratic as well as socialist principles. The real origin of the document was revealed by Bartholomew Hlapane, former Communist Party member and ANC executive member. According to Hlapane:

'The Freedom Charter is a document I came to know about having just been drafted by Joe Slovo at the request of the Central Committee of the South African Communist Party.'
('Talking With the ANC', produced by the South African Bureau of Information, 1986.)

SOURCE 121 — Nelson Mandela on the Freedom Charter
The Charter is a revolutionary document because the changes it envisages cannot be won without breaking the set-up of present South Africa.

Whilst the Charter proclaims democratic changes of a far-reaching nature, it is by no means a blueprint for a socialist state. Its declaration: 'The People Shall Govern' visualises the transfer of power to all the people of this country, be they workers, peasants, professional men or middle class.
('The Struggle Is My Life', by Nelson Mandela, IDAF Publications, 1986.)

Questions

1. In what way did the Defiance Campaign contribute to the formation of the Congress Alliance?
2. Why were appeals such as those in Source 116 issued? Is there any link between this source and the comment by the Eminent Persons Group that the Congress of the People was the most representative gathering ever held in South Africa?
3. Does the picture on page 67 confirm Bishop Huddleston's views about the mood of the Congress? Which laws did the people want changed?
4. Which aspects of the Freedom Charter would the government not agree with?
5. What is Source 120's opinion of the Charter? Can you explain why it took such a view?
6. Nelson Mandela described the Freedom Charter as 'Revolutionary'. From your reading of Source 118 would you agree with this view?
7. How would most ordinary Africans view the Freedom Charter?

The Treason Trial

While the People's Congress was in progress it was raided by the Security Police. They were searching for evidence of treason. Every delegate was searched, many documents were confiscated and even signs advertising meals were taken away. The delegates were in a good mood and the police raid seemed to cheer them up even more.

The government had decided that it was time to put a halt to the activities of the ANC. Believing that the information it had collected was enough to convict the leaders of treason, it made a series of arrests in December 1956. Altogether 156 people were arrested in the biggest police operation yet seen in South Africa.

All the prisoners were transferred to the Fort in Johannesburg. The arrested were from every racial group in South Africa and ranged from leaders like Nelson Mandela and Albert Luthuli to ordinary South Africans: clerks, factory workers, housewives. Banning Orders had prevented people meeting each other. Now thanks to the government, the ANC leaders were all together. The charges they were facing were serious: high treason carried the death penalty.

The 156 South Africans of all races who were arrested and charged with treason. The trial began in 1956 and dragged on until 1961.

SOURCE 122 — Albert Luthuli is arrested

The police knock came; my wife admitted them and they came through to the bedroom. Warrants were produced: first a warrant for my arrest and then a search warrant. I sat down on the edge of the bed and read them through. The charge of High Treason was unexpected. In the afternoon we were flown up to Johannesburg. It was not until we had been through various formalities that we realised just how extensive the arrests were. In the cells were men from every corner of the land.

('Let My People Go', by Albert Luthuli, Fontana, 1962.)

The initial stages of the trial were chaotic. First the defendants had to appear before magistrates who had to decide if there was enough evidence to proceed with the charge of treason. When notices from Kliptown were shown which read:

'Comrades Tea 3d, Tea and Sandwich 6d' and 'Soup with Meat, Soup without Meat', there was widespread laughter.

The trial itself did not begin until 1957 and did not finish until 1961. By that time the charges against 120 defendants had been dropped. In 1960 Nelson Mandela gave evidence in which he denied the charges of treason.

In the early stages of the Treason Trial there were large demonstrations outside the courtroom.

The Treason Trial: the Government's Attempt to Silence Opposition

SOURCE 123 — Nelson Mandela's Evidence

We are not anti-white, we are against white supremacy and in this struggle we have the support of some sections of the European population.

It is quite clear that the ANC has consistently preached a policy of race harmony and we are against racialism.

Economic pressure, defiance campaigns and stay-at-home strikes would be the weapons used until the government was prepared to talk.

Between 1957 and 1960 the defendants in the trial had been released on bail, but events outside the courtroom changed the climate of the trial. The unrest following the Sharpeville Massacre led the government to introduce a State of Emergency. The leaders of the ANC were held in detention and the ANC itself was declared an illegal organisation and banned. The government hoped that by taking this action it would put a stop to the activities of the ANC. The trial ended in March 1961 and the result was a great embarrassment for the government.

SOURCE 124 — The findings of Mr Justice Rumpf

The ANC and its allies had been working to replace the government with a different form of state.

The ANC envisaged the use of illegal means and these had already been used during the Defiance Campaign.

Certain leaders made speeches inciting violence, but the state had failed to prove a policy of violence.

The state had not proved that the ANC was communist nor that the Freedom Charter pictured a communist state.

SOURCE 125 — Winnie Mandela describes events after the trial

At the end of the Treason Trial in 1961, Nelson came home with other members of the outlawed ANC and he simply said:

'Oh darling, just pack a few things for me in a suitcase.'

He was outside the gate, but I couldn't reach him as there were so many people wishing him well — everybody was excited. I packed his bag, but by the time I took it out he wasn't there.

In the papers on the following day I read that he had emerged in Pietermaritzburg and addressed a convention I knew nothing about. I had not even realised his Banning Order had expired.

That was the last I saw of my husband as a family man, legally at home.
('Part of My Soul' by Winnie Mandela, Penguin Books, 1985.)

The verdict of the trial was a victory for the ANC and a humiliation for the government. Events had caught up with the ANC and the political situation in South Africa was now very different from what it had been at the time the trial started. The government hoped that by banning the ANC they would no longer find it a problem. The leaders were faced with a choice: to obey the government and give up the struggle or to continue illegally underground. In December 1960, before the trial had ended, leaders of the ANC had decided to continue the struggle.

Questions

1. Were the treason trial defendants arrested just because of their involvement in the Congress of the People, or was their arrest linked to other protests?
2. What do the number of those arrested and the charges suggest about the government's attitude to the ANC?
3. Nelson Mandela claimed in court that the ANC was not anti-white. Does the picture on page 69 prove this claim?
4. Why did the activities of the ANC not amount to treason?
5. Was the verdict of the trial a victory for the ANC?

Sharpeville

This chapter deals with the following topics:
1. The split between the ANC and the Pan African Congress.
2. The Anti-Pass Law Campaign.
3. The events surrounding the Sharpeville Massacre in March 1960.
4. How the massacre affected other events in South Africa and the rest of the world.

After reading this chapter and completing the exercises you will have:
1. Looked at different accounts of the massacre.
2. Seen that the massacre was a turning point in the campaign against apartheid laws.
3. Examined the consequences of the massacre inside South Africa.
4. Examined the consequences of the massacre for South Africa's relations with the rest of the world.

In 1960 the treason trial had still not finished. It was having a serious effect on the ANC. Some of the leaders had to attend the court every day and others, like Chief Albert Luthuli, were 'banned'. Luthuli could not communicate with other ANC members or be involved in any political activity. Some members of the ANC grew impatient with their leaders. They thought that they were not active enough. The biggest disagreement was over the future of South Africa. The ANC wanted a country where all people in South Africa were equal — black, coloured, Asian and white — and they welcomed any support, even from the South African Communist Party.

A sizeable group objected to this policy; they thought that Communism was a foreign idea, but the most important disagreement was over the idea of 'Africanism'. They believed that Africa was for the Africans and that the whites and other non-African groups had no right to have power or influence in South Africa. Eventually these people broke away from the ANC and formed their own group, the Pan Africanist Congress, whose aim was 'government of the African by the African for the African.' Their leader was Robert Sobukwe. The ANC did not want the Africanists to break away; they thought that this action would weaken the opposition to apartheid.

Robert Sobukwe, leader of the Pan African Congress. The PAC was an offshoot of the ANC. Its members did not approve of the multi-racial policies of the ANC and complained about the influence of Communists inside the ANC. The PAC organised an anti-pass law demonstration in March 1960 which led to the Sharpeville Massacre. Like the ANC, the PAC was banned, following the unrest after Sharpeville.

SOURCE 126 — Albert Luthuli explains his objections to the ideas of the PAC

The co-operation between people of different race is one of the most hopeful advances of the last twelve years, not merely because it increases the impact of resistance but because it is the beginning of a non-racial South Africa. In the long run the PAC policy will obstruct the way to a South Africa which embraces all her citizens.

◄ What did Albert Luthuli mean when he said: 'Co-operation between people of different races is one of the most hopeful advances'?

At the beginning of 1960 both the ANC and the PAC were organising the next stage of their protest against apartheid. They aimed to campaign against the Pass Laws.

SOURCE 127 — Preparations for the Pass Law Campaign

It was our intention not to launch the new campaign until our people were thoroughly ready to participate. But the PAC had also in mind a programme of action against the passes. Their method was to go to police stations, leaving their passes at home, and asked to be arrested. Taking the country as a whole they were organised only in a few centres. Robert Sobukwe called on all Africans to follow him in leaving their passes at home. His call cut across ANC plans for an orderly, carefully mounted campaign with a deliberately timed climax.

The PAC campaign began on the morning of 21 March 1960, when Robert Sobukwe and other leaders of the PAC presented themselves for arrest in Johannesburg. The police in most places handled the demonstrations with tact and good humour. Leaders were arrested, but others were told to go home. In Sharpeville, to the south of Johannesburg, the demonstration went disastrously wrong.

The Sharpeville Massacre — Using the Evidence

On the following pages newspaper reports describe the events surrounding the shootings and the aftermath of the massacre.

Before the Massacre

Crowds gathering in Sharpeville on the morning of March 21, 1960. When looking at this photograph, the accounts of the police witness about the size and mood of the crowd should also be taken into account.

SOURCE 128 — Times, Tuesday, 22 March 1960

Around Vereeniging trouble was apparently expected; there was shooting in the morning in which one African was killed and another seriously wounded.

After the shooting in the morning police reinforcements were sent there. Soon after noon about a dozen Saracen armoured vehicles were on call at the Sharpeville location. Soon the police station at Sharpeville, standing in a large open compound, was virtually beseiged by thousands of Africans shouting, 'Africa, Africa.'

The only way police could make contact with those inside the station was to force a way in with the Saracens. As soon as the armoured cars got through the ranks of the Africans would close again. A council motor car which went through earlier in the morning emerged as a wreck, with the occupants injured. Gradually the station force was built up to 60 armed police men.

SOURCE 129 — Guardian, Tuesday, 22 March 1960
The Pan Africanist Congress had called on their members to come without their passes and surrender themselves for arrest at the nearest police station.

Sharpeville police station was literally besieged by thousands of African men and women and police could only make contact with it by forcing their way through with Saracen armoured cars. Aircraft which dived low over the area in an attempt to disperse the crowd seemed to anger the Africans. The first African was shot dead and four Africans and several policemen were injured after the police had been stoned. The Africans retaliated, causing casualties amongst the police.

◀ In what way do Sources 128 and 129
 (a) agree
and
 (b) disagree about the events in Sharpeville during the morning of 20 March 1960?
◀ Do the pictures on page 73 and below support any of the statements made in Sources 128 and 129?

Crowds at Sharpeville at midday. Again, refer to the police reports about the mood of the crowd and difficulties for police cars to move in the area around the police station. The 'thumbs up' sign was a traditional protest sign. Look back at the pictures on pages 69 and 70.

The Sharpeville Massacre: Using the Evidence I

The Shooting

Bodies in the street after the shooting.

SOURCE 130 — Times, Tuesday, 22 March 1960

Quite suddenly there were bursts of firing, chiefly from sten guns (machine guns), and the mob scattered leaving about 80 people sprawled on the ground in a growing pool of blood. Among them was a dead child and a screaming woman, painfully if superficially wounded. By dusk a dozen bodies were in the mortuary with, according to the police, more to come in. Some 30 people had been admitted to hospital with serious wounds.

One report put the number of dead at more than 50 while the injured people exceeded 150, including a score of women and children.

Mr Charles Channor, a press photographer with long war experience described the scene as the 'bloodiest' he had ever seen; he added that most of the young constables were 'obviously appalled' by what their shooting had done and they tried to make amends by the 'almost frenzy' with which they helped to get the wounded people into ambulances.

SOURCE 131 — Guardian, Tuesday, 22 March 1960

56 Africans including women and children were killed and 162 wounded when South African Police opened fire on the crowd.

The police opened fire with sub-machine guns, sten guns and rifles and eye-witnesses said that the front ranks of the crowd fell like nine pins. The crowd then retreated, leaving their dead and wounded in the street.

Mangled bodies of men, women and children lay sprawled on the roadway in the square. One policeman described the scene as 'like a battlefield'. A Johannesburg news photographer, whose car was riddled with bullets, said he had taken more pictures of bloodshed than he had ever seen before in South Africa.

The South African Press Assocation said one police officer instructed an African to collect pieces of mangled body in a hat with a shovel and then spread sand over pools of blood in Sharpeville Road.

Scenes after the shooting when, according to police reports, the officers hurriedly tried to get the injured to hospital.

The Sharpeville Massacre: Using the Evidence II

An African woman lies dead after the shooting. From the position of the body it would appear that she had been shot in the back.

◀ In Sources 130, 131 and 132 there is no agreement about the number of people killed and wounded. Why might there be this discrepancy? Will this affect the reliability of any of the Sources?

◀ In Source 130 one of the witnesses claims that the police were 'appalled' and that they were 'trying to make amends'. Do the pictures on page 75 confirm this view of the police behaviour after the shooting?

◀ People say that 'the camera cannot lie'. How reliable does this make the pictures on page 75 and the one above as pieces of evidence?

Burial of the victims of the Sharpeville Massacre.

SOURCE 132 — The Government response: Times, Tuesday 22 March 1960

Dr Verwoerd gave Parliament details of the disorders. He said that some 2,000 Africans demonstrated by entering people's homes and forcibly removing identity books.

The crowd gradually grew until there were some 20,000. Telephone wires were cut and disturbances occurred. The police had to open fire and 25 people were killed and 50 wounded. Dr Verwoerd said these facts and figures were provisional.

SOURCE 133 — Times, Wednesday, 23 March 1960

Dr Verwoerd, who was replying to a debate on yesterday's rioting, said his first duty was to thank the South African police on behalf of the House and the people for the courageous, efficient way they handled the situation. The police at times found it difficult to control themselves, but they had done so in an exemplary manner.

From some speeches in the House, he said, there might have been a suggestion that the police used excessive force; but the suggestion was not definite and he would rather not reply to it.

SOURCE 134 — Guardian, Tuesday, 22 March, 1960

'I don't know how many we shot,' said Colonel J Piernaar, the local police commander at Sharpeville. 'It all started when hordes of natives surrounded the police station. My car was struck by a stone. If they do these things they must learn their lessons the hard way.'

SOURCE 135 — Times, Saturday, 26 March 1960

A statement issued last night from South Africa House in London said that the demonstrators at Sharpeville fired first and the police were forced to fire in self-defence.

As to the factual information now available the disturbances at Sharpeville on Monday resulted from planned demonstrations of about 20,000 natives in which the demonstrators attacked the police with assorted weapons, including firearms.

The demonstrators shot first and the police were forced to fire in self-defence to avoid even more tragic results. The allegations of the Afro-Asian group in the United Nations in requesting a Security Council meeting because the demonstrators were unarmed and peaceful were therefore completely untrue. As recently as January 24th, nine policemen (4 white and 5 non-white) were brutally battered to death by a so-called "unarmed mob of native rioters near Durban". A full judicial inquiry is being instituted to establish all the relevant facts.

The Sharpeville Massacre: Using the Evidence III

SOURCE 136 — What really happened, Guardian, Saturday, 26 March 1960

The Anglican Bishop of Johannesburg, Ambrose Reeves, has accused the South African Government of showing a complete lack of compassion for the bloodshed at Sharpeville.

The statement he issued was mainly taken from sworn affidavits (statements) from those wounded at Sharpeville.

All the affidavits, he said, contradicted the government claim that the Police Station was besieged by 20,000 Africans. A figure supported by European witnesses to the shooting said that the crowd was no more than 4,000.

The affidavits showed that the European police lined up outside the police station and all fired together. All the affidavits maintain that the crowd was not armed — even with sticks. The police acted together in raising their weapons, aiming and firing. (Dr Verwoerd has said that no order was given for the police to open fire.)

The affidavits showed that the white police did not attempt to give a warning before opening fire. The only warning came from an African policeman who rushed towards the fence shouting 'Run, they are going to shoot.' At that moment the police opened fire.

The Bishop said that the overwhelming number of those being treated at the hospital had been wounded in the back.

All the affidavits insisted that the crowd was entirely good natured and unarmed and did not converge on the police station with violent intentions.

The desperate physical condition of many of the wounded and the fact that they were in separate wards ruled out the possibility of collaboration on their stories told to the lawyers taking affidavits.

SOURCE 137 — Summary of the findings of the Judicial Inquiry

1. The size of the crowd was disputed; police evidence claimed that the crowd was around 20,000. Other witnesses claimed that it was no more than 5,000.
2. The police evidence claimed that the crowd was in a violent and hostile mood.
3. Charles Channor claimed that the crowd was in a holiday mood, singing and laughing but noisy.
4. Captain Pienaar claimed that he could only force a way through the hostile crowd with great difficulty in armoured cars .
5. Another police officer claimed to have no difficulty and said that many people were just sitting on the side of the road.

The judge concluded that the police had deliberately suppressed the evidence. *(contd.)*

Pienaar was an experienced police officer and should have considered other means of dispersing the crowd, for example a baton charge.

Pienaar had claimed that such methods would be useless; he said:

'The native mentality does not allow Africans to gather for peaceful demonstrations. For them to gather means violence!'

This forced the judge to conclude that the police regarded the Africans as a mob and not as 'human beings'.

The quantity of ammunition used and the type of wounds received — mostly in the back, proved that the firing had been indiscriminate.

He had no alternative but to conclude that the shootings were deliberate and unnecessary.

The inquiry was impartial and had established what many people had already suspected. Unfortunately the results of the inquiry were largely irrelevant. Events had overtaken the slow-moving offical inquiry. Whatever the report said, it had no effect on the black opposition.

Questions

1. In what ways do Sources 132, 133, 134 and 135 attempt to justify the police action?
2. Are these accounts likely to be reliable?
3. How do the statements of African witnesses in Source 136 contradict the police and Government's version given in Sources 132, 133, 134 and 135?
4. Are the affidavits in Source 136 likely to be more or less reliable than Sources 132, 133, 134 and 135?
5. Do the findings of the Judicial Inquiry in Source 137 support the claims made by the police or those made by the victims of the shooting?
6. What were the most important points made in the evidence given in Sources 136 and 137?

The Sharpeville Massacre: The Aftermath

The shootings at Sharpeville were followed by a similar incident at Langa township in the Eastern Cape. The action of the South African police in killing so many of its citizens in what appeared to be cold blood shocked and angered people throughout the world. Inside South Africa black anger was so fierce that the government feared widespread unrest. It imposed a State of Emergency; the Treason Trial defendants and many other anti-apartheid protestors were detained without trial.

SOURCE 138 — Nelson Mandela's reaction to the Sharpeville Massacre

How many more Sharpevilles would there be in the history of our country? And how many more Sharpevilles could the country stand without violence and terror becoming the order of the day? And what would happen to our people when that stage was reached? In the long run we felt certain that we must succeed but at what cost to ourselves and the rest of the country. And if this happened how could black and white ever live together again in peace and harmony? These were the problems that faced us.
('The Struggle is My Life', by Nelson Mandela, IDAF Publications, 1986.)

SOURCE 139 — Albert Luthuli and the ANC response to Sharpeville

I called for a national day of mourning on the 28th March, for the victims and their families. On this day I asked people to stay at home and treat it as a day of prayer. The response was good. Moreover it was multi-racial and went far beyond our usual allies. Many churches were open throughout the land, and students of all races participated in the mourning.

But passive mourning and prayer seemed to the ANC leadership to be not enough. The Pass system had claimed more victims. Congress called for the burning of passes. We desired not to leave our shackles at home. We desired to be rid of them. I burned my Reference Book, others burned theirs, and the bonfires began to grow in number.
('Let My People Go', Albert Luthuli, Collins Fontana, 1962.)

As part of the protests against the massacre, Africans were encouraged to burn their pass books. Albert Luthuli publicly burnt his as a challenge to the government. In the days following the shootings, a State of Emergency was imposed by the government and thousands of ANC and PAC members were detained without trial.

In response to the crisis the government took two contradictory steps. The first was expected. Under the terms of the State of Emergency 20,000 known activists were detained and the ANC and the PAC declared banned organisations. The second step was the suspension of the Pass Laws. There was a faint hope that something had been achieved, but the suspension was only temporary.

Sharpeville — The Reaction of the World

The massacre brought to the world's attention more dramatically the realities of apartheid. The United Nations issued its strongest condemnation yet of apartheid and the South African government. Fearing that the massacre was just the beginning of more serious

BLACK TIDE

The cartoonist here shows Verwoerd as a modern-day King Canute, the 11th century English king who tried unsuccessfully to show how powerful he was by ordering back the tide.
(The 'Guardian', 25th March, 1960)

unrest, foreign businessmen began to take their money out of South Africa. Between 1960 and 1961, 248 million Rand was dis-invested. In the four years before 1960 foreign withdrawals only amounted to 20 million Rand.

The strongest criticism of South Africa came from the Commonwealth. Apartheid was an insult to many of the newly independent African and Asian states. Either South Africa had to go or they would leave the Commonwealth. At the Commonwealth Conference in 1961 Verwoerd was surprised by the hostility. Rather than face the humiliation of being expelled, Verwoerd announced that South Africa was leaving of her own free will.

SOURCE 140 — The Commonwealth reaction

Verwoerd's appearance may have impressed British television audiences, but both they and the Commonwealth Prime Ministers remained unimpressed at his attempts to describe apartheid as a policy of good neighbourliness. Nehru of India and Nkrumah of Ghana wanted South Africa out of the Commonwealth. Macmillan tried his best to achieve a compromise, but it was not good enough for the anti-South African lobby.

Verwoerd informed the Conference that he was withdrawing South Africa's application to remain a member of the Commonwealth saying:

I am sure that the great majority of the people of my country will appreciate that no other course was open to us. I must admit that I was amazed and shocked by the spirit of hostility and vindictiveness towards South Africa. What has happend in London was not a defeat but a victory. We have freed ourselves from the Afro-Asian states.
('The White Tribe of Africa', David Harrison, BBC Publications, 1981.)

SOURCE 141 — World reaction to Sharpeville

Most significant was the resolution tabled at the fifteenth session of the United Nations which called for sanctions against South Africa. This had the support of all the African members of the UN except one. The significance was not minimised by the fact that a milder resolution was finally adopted calling for individual sanctions. The following year the African states played a marvellous role in calling for the expulsion of South Africa from the United Nations. This increasing world pressure on South Africa has greatly weakened her international position and given a boost to the freedom struggle inside the country.
(Nelson Mandela: speech to the Pan-African Freedom Conference, Addis Ababa, January 1962. From his book 'The Struggle is My Life', IDAF Publications, 1986.)

Questions

1. From Source 138 what dangers did Nelson Mandela foresee if the authorities continued to react to African protests as they had done at Sharpeville?
2. In the light of Nelson Mandela's fears how reasonable were the protests which Albert Luthuli describes in Source 139?
3. Verwoerd said that he was shocked by the hostility of other Commonwealth members in Source 140. Why were they so hostile?
4. What message is the cartoonist trying to convey in the cartoon at the top of the page? Does the information in Sources 140 and 141 add to your understanding of this cartoon?
5. Was Nelson Mandela pleased with the measures taken by other nations of the world?

Umkhonto We Sizwe

This chapter deals with the following topics:
1. How Umkhonto came to be created.
2. What Umkhonto wanted to achieve.
3. The trial of the leaders of Umkhonto.
4. The evidence against Nelson Mandela.

After reading this chapter and completing the exercises you will have:
1. Discovered the reasons for the creation of Umkhonto.
2. Seen that Umkhonto was a new stage in the opposition to apartheid.
3. Examined the trial evidence to help you answer the question — 'Is Nelson Mandela a communist?'

When the treason trial ended in 1961 the defendants were found not guilty. Nelson Mandela, with other leaders of the ANC, began to organise the next stage of their campaign against apartheid. They demanded that the government should arrange a National Convention, a meeting where all the different groups in South Africa could meet and talk about the future of the country.

Not surprisingly, the government refused. In protest the ANC organised a stay-at-home in May 1961. The idea was that supporters would refuse to go to work for three days and stay in their homes. It was thought that this tactic would keep people away from the police and army and avoid bloodshed. The government said that the stay-at-home was illegal and over 10,000 Africans were arrested. Despite this, the demonstration went ahead. The government called out the army, expecting trouble. For two days most Blacks, Asians and Coloureds stayed away from work; business and industry were badly affected.

Despite this success, the ANC called off the action after the second day. In a statement issued by Nelson Mandela it was clear that the mood of the ANC was changing. They saw that their peaceful protests had no effect on the government. A new phase in the struggle for human rights in South Africa was about to begin. This was to be an important turning point. In December 1961 there were several explosions throughout South Africa. Electricity pylons and other 'economic' targets were blown up. Responsibility for the attacks was claimed by a new organisation — Umkhonto We Sizwe (the Spear of the Nation).

SOURCE 142 — Nelson Mandela explains why the ANC felt justified in abandoning the policy of non-violence
The stay-at-home was to be peaceful . . . careful instructions were given to avoid any violence. The government's answer was to introduce harsher laws and to send soldiers into the townships to intimidate the people.

◄ Why did the stay-at-home finally convince the ANC that it was time to change their tactics?

We had no doubt that we had to continue the fight. The problem was how. The hard facts were that fifty years of non-violence had brought the African people nothing but fewer and fewer rights. I and some colleagues came to the conclusion that it would be wrong for African leaders to continue preaching non-violence when the government met our peaceful demands with force.

SOURCE 143 — The Manifesto of Umkhonto We Sizwe

Units of Umkhonto today carried out planned attacks against government installations.

Umkhonto will carry out the struggle for freedom by new methods.

The main liberation movements in this country have consistently followed a policy of non-violence. But the people's patience is not endless.

There comes a time in the life of any nation when there remain only two choices: submit or fight.

That time has now come in South Africa.

Umkhonto will be the fighting arm of the people against the government.

We hope that we will bring the government to its senses before it is too late so that both the government and its policies can be changed before matters reach the desperate stage of civil war.

SOURCE 144 — The South African Government's account of the formation of Umkhonto

The ANC and PAC were banned, but new underground organisations took their place. Umkhonto was established in 1961 by Nelson Mandela and other ANC leaders for sabotage operations in preparation for the commencement of guerilla warfare.

Electric pylons blown up by Umkhonto We Sizwe. These were typical of the kind of targets attacked. In his trial Nelson Mandela maintained that their aim was sabotage and targets were chosen where the risk of killing people was small.

Umkhonto We Sizwe: The Motives of a New Opposition Group

After the treason trial, Nelson Mandela went into hiding. He went all over South Africa speaking secretly at meetings encouraging his supporters. Mandela gained a reputation as a daring underground figure, managing to keep one step ahead of the police. In 1962 he left South Africa and travelled around Africa and Europe seeking support for the ANC and Umkhonto. In August 1962 Mandela was finally caught and put on trial for leaving the country illegally.

SOURCE 145 — Nelson Mandela explains why he went underground

I am informed that the police are looking for me, I will not give myself up to a government I do not recognise. I have chosen this course which is more difficult and which entails more risk and hardship. I have had to separate myself from my dear wife and children, from my mother and sisters, to live as an outlaw in my own land. I have had to abandon my profession and live in poverty, as many people are doing. The struggle is my life.

SOURCE 146 — Winnie Mandela describes meeting her husband while he was underground

We had a very dramatic life. I waited for the knock on the window in the early hours of the morning. They were watching me twenty four hours a day and I had to slip out past the police to go to him.

Someone would come and order me to follow him in my car. We would drive a kilometre or so, we would then meet another car, we would jump from that into another and by the time I reached him I had gone through something like ten cars. I never knew where he was, his hideouts were all over the country.

The arrest of Walter Sisulu and other leaders of the ANC at Rivonia was a blow to the movement. Some of the most important leaders had been arrested. Documents found at Rivonia revealed the links between the ANC and Umkhonto and Nelson Mandela's role in the foundation of Umkhonto. The arrested were charged under the Suppression of Communism Act and the Sabotage Act. If found guilty they would face the death penalty.

The Rivonia Trial: Is Nelson Mandela a Communist? An Examination of the Evidence

In October 1963 Nelson Mandela, Walter Sisulu and eight other members of Umkhonto were brought to trial. Between them they were accused of being responsible for 196 separate acts of sabotage, of recruiting people for sabotage with the aim of causing a violent revolution. The accused did not deny belonging to Umkhonto or the acts of sabotage. The other charges claimed that Nelson Mandela was a Communist and that the ANC was a Communist organisation.

Daily **RAND** Mail FINAL

JOHANNESBURG, SATURDAY, JULY 13, 1963   Price 3 cents

Police swoop on Rand sparks huge investigation
LUXURY HOUSE COMBED

Documents taken after 18 arrests

By CHRIS VERMAAK
Crime Reporter

P OLICE yesterday combed every inch of the secluded luxury country house in Johannesburg's outlying northern suburb of Rivonia, where 18 people were detained by security police on Thursday night. The arrests have sparked off country-wide investigations.

Apart from apparatus and documents confiscated soon after the arrests, yesterday's search revealed important data, typewriters and other articles.

Police said that it would take them weeks to study all the documents, including those found in the house of Mr. Lionel Bernstein, one of the detained men.

Police would not disclose what articles had been confiscated. Asked if radio equipment was included among confiscated articles, during the raid which a senior police officer described as an important roundup, he said no further information could be divulged.

A facsimile of newspaper headlines announcing the capture of Umkhonto leaders at Rivonia outside Johannesburg. The documents found at the farmhouse were to prove vital for the prosecution.

SOURCE 147 — The South African Government claims that Mandela is a Communist

The full extent of the Rivonia leaders' plans to overthrow the government by violent means was revealed during the trial. Several articles in Mandela's handwriting were submitted to the court including articles on 'How to be a good Communist' and 'Political Economy'. In the latter document Mandela wrote:

'We Communist party members are the most advanced revolutionaries in modern history.'

SOURCE 148 — Further evidence presented by the Government against Nelson Mandela

A notepad containing 18 pages in Mandela's handwriting was another of the documentary exhibits. One of the passages read:

'The people of South Africa, led by the South African Communist Party, will destroy capitalist society and build in its place socialism. This cannot be brought about by slow change or by reforms, as liberals often advise, but by revolution. One must therefore be a revolutionary and not a reformer.'

SOURCE 149 — Nelson Mandela explains the evidence against him

The three exhibits in my handwriting were notes that I once had made. An old friend who was a member of the Communist Party had been trying to persuade me to join the Communist Party. I made repeated refusals and criticised communist literature for being full of jargon. The friend had asked me to re-write them in simpler form. I agreed but I never finished the task; I never again saw the notepad until it was produced at the trial.

SOURCE 150 — Nelson Mandela deals with the accusation that he and the ANC are part of the Communist Party

I have always regarded myself as an African patriot. I have been influenced by communist thought. But this is true of many of the leaders of the new independent states. Such different persons as Gandhi and Nkrumah. We all accept the need for some form of socialism to enable our people to catch up with the advanced countries of this world. This does not mean that we are communists.

I have been influenced in my thinking by both east and west. I must leave myself free to borrow the best from the west and the east. The suggestion made by the state that the struggle in South Africa is under the influence of foreigners or communists is incorrect.

Is Nelson Mandela a Communist? An Examination of the Evidence

SOURCE 151 — Nelson Mandela's final statement from the dock at the Rivonia Trial

During my lifetime I have dedicated myself to the struggle of the African people. I have fought against white domination and I have fought against black domination. I have cherished the ideal of a democratic and free society in which all persons live together in harmony and with equal opportunities. It is an ideal which I hope to live for and to achieve. But if needs be, it is an ideal for which I am prepared to die.

Nelson Mandela and Walter Sisulu on Robben Island. This is the last photograph of Nelson Mandela. The Rivonia defendants, with the exception of Dennis Goldberg who was white, were first imprisoned on Robben Island, a bleak rocky outcrop in Table Bay, Cape Town.

SOURCE 152 — Albert Luthuli's press statement issued on behalf of the ANC at the end of the Rivonia Trial

The ANC held to a policy of using non-violent means of struggle.

In the face of the white refusal to abandon a policy which denies the African freedom no-one can blame brave and just men for seeking justice by the use of violent methods in order to ultimately establish peace and racial harmony. They believe in justice and when they are locked away justice will have departed from the South African scene.

In June 1964 the trial ended; eight of the ten accused were found guilty. The judge agreed that Umkhonto attacks were against property and not people. The defendants were sentenced to life imprisonment and the judge said that the life sentences should mean exactly that.

The world press condemned the sentences. The London *Times* said that the wrong people had been on trial and the *New York Times* said that the Rivonia defendants were the George Washingtons and Benjamin Franklins of South Africa.

SOURCE 153 — The Commonwealth Eminent Persons Group assesses the significant part which Nelson Mandela has to play in the future of South Africa

Mr Mandela is a unifying and popular leader. Our personal observations revealed that blacks, Indians and coloureds look to Nelson Mandela as the leader of a non-racial South Africa. His freedom is a key part in any hope of a peaceful solution.

That he is a nationalist cannot be denied; but of his supposed communism, either now or in the past, we found no trace. In that respect we differ from the Government which has resorted to the most dubious methods to denigrate his reputation.

Nelson Mandela remains in prison to this day. Despite being isolated for twenty-five years, he is still an important figure in South Africa. Many blacks still see him as their leader. His release is demanded by many groups inside and outside South Africa as a sign that the government is genuine in its desire to seek a peaceful end to the unrest.

Questions

1. In what ways is Source 143 a consequence of decisions taken in Source 142?
2. Why was this said to be a turning point in black opposition?
3. Source 144 claims that the aim of Umkhonto was to start guerilla warfare: what evidence
   a. supports this claim?
   b. contradicts this claim.
   Can you explain the different views of Umkhonto's actions?
4. At the trial the accused admitted being involved in sabotage; the prosecution therefore spent most of its time trying to prove that Mandela and others were communists. What evidence supports the prosecution claim?
5. Using Sources 149, 150 and 151 how did Mandela answer these accusations? Can we believe his evidence?
6. Sources 146, 147 and 148 are from a South African Government publication entitled *Talking With the ANC,* published in 1986. Does this fact affect the reliability of the evidence?
7. What is the significance of the assessment of Nelson Mandela made in 1986 by the Commonwealth Eminent Persons Group?

Soweto 1976

This chapter deals with the following topics:
1. The rise of the Black Consciousness Movement.
2. The unrest in Soweto and other townships.
3. The reaction to the unrest
   a. In South Africa
   b. In the rest of the world.

After reading this chapter and completing the exercises you will have:
1. Discovered what is meant by Black Consciousness.
2. Examined the part played by the Black Consciousness movement in the 1970s.
3. Examined the causes of the unrest.
4. Seen that the violence in the townships had important results in South Africa and the wider world.

After the imprisonment of the Rivonia defendants in 1964 the South African government thought that it had broken the back of African opposition to apartheid. The Nationalists believed that apartheid was a success: non-whites in South Africa knew their place and the Afrikaner was in command. Towards the end of the 1960s a new movement began to win support amongst the Africans. It was similar to the Black Power Movement in the United States; in South Africa it was called Black Consciousness. Its aim was to give black South Africans confidence in themselves, to restore their pride and make them realise that they had the power to change their position in South Africa.

One of the leaders of Black Consciousness was a young medical student from the Eastern Cape, Steve Biko. Biko helped to create the South African Students Organisation, SASO. The multi-racial National Union of South African Students at first opposed SASO. They saw it as a form of self-imposed apartheid. By 1972 there were several Black Consciousness groups that were united under the Black Peoples' Convention.

One important way in which these organisations worked was with ordinary Africans in their neighbourhoods. They organised and ran community centres, advice bureaux and training centres. Black consciousness placed a great deal of importance on being part of the community. It was inevitable that the activities of the BPC came to the attention of the authorities. Leaders were often arrested, harassed, banned and imprisoned.

Steve Biko speaking at a Black Consciousness meeting. Black Consciousness tried to give Africans confidence in themselves to change their way of life.

SOURCE 154 — The aims of Black Consciousness
The bulk of the black people have accepted their status. Status is determined at birth and for life by colour. The black person has been uprooted and pursued.

I believe that we have values and standards which are different from whites.

The first step therefore is to make the black man see himself, to pump life into his empty shell, to fill him with pride and dignity.

This means that black people must build a position of non-dependence on whites.

Black man you are on your own!

('Biko' by Donald Woods, Penguin Books, 1979.)

◄ What do you understand by the term 'Black Consciousness'? Are there any similarities between Black Consciousness and the ideas of Robert Sobukwe?

In 1976 the government announced that certain subjects in schools would be taught in Afrikaans. Officials in the Ministry of Education had warned politicians that such a move would be widely resented, but the government insisted that its plans should go ahead. African pupils, many of whom were members of SASO, objected to this plan, as did teachers and parents. They regarded Afrikaans as the language of their enemy and it was a language they were not familiar with. To be forced to learn in Afrikaans would put the pupils at a disadvantage. On 16 June 1976 SASO organised a march through the streets of Soweto to protest about the decision.

Soweto Eye-Witnesses Give Evidence

SOURCE 155 — The events of 16 June in Soweto

The police came out of cars and advanced towards us, a white policeman threw tear gas. We dispersed and then came back. We thought they would speak to us through a loudhailer. The same white policeman opened fire on the students.

I was with Hector Peterson. He was the first student I saw go down. I saw him being shot in the head. When Hector was shot the students ran back. I was feeling scared, I wanted to run away. The policeman was aiming his gun at Hector again wanting to finish him off. This girl stood in front of the police and told them in Afrikaans: 'shoot for me'. He shot in the air.

(Tsietsi Mashinini, President of the Soweto Students Council.)

This was the scene in Soweto on 16 June 1976 as students marched to protest against the imposition of Afrikaans as a language in black schools.

SOURCE 156

Λ white policeman without warning hurled a tear gas canister into the crowd which immediately began throwing rocks and other missiles at the police. Miss Tema then saw a white policeman pull out his revolver and fire it. Other police joined in firing into the crowd. She took a child aged about seven to a near-by clinic but he was dead on arrival.
(Statement by Sophie Tema, a black newspaper reporter who was standing behind police lines.)

SOURCE 157 — The scale of destruction in Soweto

Twenty buildings mostly belonging to the government were on fire and many cars were overturned and burnt out. A Johannesburg fire engine was hijacked by rioters.
(Guardian, 17 June 1976.)

After a night of relative calm the students, now joined by adults, set fire to cars and buildings. More schools and public buildings were razed.

There were nasty scenes in the centre of Johannesburg as 500 students from the white University of Witwatersrand marched through the streets with posters proclaiming 'Why shoot black children' and 'Black Education Kills'. The marchers were dispersed by baton wielding policemen.
(Guardian, 18 June 1976.)

The Johannesburg student rebellion spilled out of Soweto and spread violently into at least seven other townships in the Rand.

The Army is ready to take over key points,' said Brigadier J Visser Deputy Chief of Police in Johannesburg. 'The situation was deteriorating but I have all the support I need and would use sterner methods from now on.'
(Guardian, 19 June 1976.)

Questions

1. According to Sources 155 and 156 how did the violence begin?
2. Did all white South Africans believe Kruger or approve of the actions of the security forces? What evidence is there to support your answer?
3. According to Source 157 what were the main targets of the Africans? Can you suggest why these particular targets were singled out for attack?

Soweto: The Reactions

The demands of the students were simple at the start of the unrest: no teaching in Afrikaans. As the riots continued and more lost their lives the demands of the students became more general. They wanted all those arrested to be released and, perhaps most important, an end to apartheid. They asked their parents to stay at home and not go to work. Many parents thought that this was the least that they could do after all that their children had been through.

A Black Parents Association was formed in Soweto which attempted to mediate between the police and the children. The call for a stay-at-home provoked violence between migrant workers living in hostels in Soweto and the other residents. Many were killed in these clashes and more than once the police looked the other way.

The unrest which began in Soweto gathered pace. Soon there were violent clashes in most large townships and the centre of Cape Town itself was transformed into a battlefield, as police used tear gas, bird shot and sjamboks to disperse black, white and coloured demonstrators. The unrest in 1976 was unlike anything seen before in South Africa. It was not until October 1976 that the authorities could claim that they had ended the disturbances.

SOURCE 158 — The demands of the students

For the scrapping of Bantu Education.

For the release of all persons detained during the demonstrations.

For the overthrow of oppression.

We, the students of Soweto, call on our parents to stay at home and not to go to work from Monday.

Our slogan is:
Away with Vorster!
Down with oppression!
Power to the people!
(Poster issued by the students in Soweto one week after the first riots.)

SOURCE 159 — The Government reaction

The Justice Minister Mr James Kruger said tonight (16 June) that the police did everything in their power to bring the students under control and were eventually forced to fire warning shots over their heads.

Mr Kruger made an appeal for peace asking blacks to accept the good faith of whites. He said he had every reason to expect there had been some organising factor behind the rioting. A certain section of blacks was seeking confrontation with whites. His target is the black consciousness movement SASO and SASM (South African Schools Movement).

Mr Kruger said he had been expecting the outbreak for some time. That was why he had recently armed himself with the new Internal Security Laws providing for indefinite internment without trial. Asked why police had not used rubber bullets, Mr Kruger said that after investigation it had been found that they made the people 'Tame to the gun'. Rioters must know that when a policeman picks up a rifle the best thing to do is get out of the way.

The role of agitators had been played down by opposition groups. A comment in the *Tribune* today said:

'The agitators are poverty, frustration and the cruel jaws of apartheid.'

Hector Peterson was one of the first children to be killed on 16 June. There were to be many others. The shootings in Soweto sparked off a wave of rioting and unrest throughout South Africa's black Township.

The events of 1976 were totally different from the shootings in Sharpeville. Television crews from around the world reported on events live from the Townships. The scale of the unrest and the methods of the South African police were seen by millions — except in South Africa. Newspapers worldwide printed the photograph of thirteen-year-old Hector Peterson on their front pages (see left).

As student protests spread throughout black Townships Brigadier Visser promised to respond with sterner measures. Thousands were arrested and many more were to die before the unrest ended in October.

SOURCE 160 — Why Soweto was different — an African view

After Sharpeville — unlike now — there was not the determination to fight. The students are taking the lead but have the majority of the adult population behind them. Are we to stop now when so many of our children have died for us? The gunning down of our children has sharpened our anger. Now that every parent is involved they want to see that their children have not died in vain.
(Oshadi Phakathi, National President of the Young Women's Christian Association, detained during the Soweto unrest.)

Worldwide criticism of South Africa was inevitable. The disgust which many felt did not die down as it had after Sharpeville. In many countries in the West anti-apartheid groups put pressure on governments and organised demonstrations. Multi-national Companies like Ford and Shell, which had factories in South Africa, expressed concern and money began to be taken out of South Africa. There were calls from the United Nations and the Organisation of African Unity (OAU) for sanctions against the government in Pretoria. In 1977 the United Nations imposed a ban on the sale of arms to South Africa.

SOURCE 161 — The OAU calls for sanctions

The OAU is threatening to call an African boycott of the Montreal Olympics if New Zealand is allowed to compete. This move is intended to isolate South Africa and countries linked with her in any way.

Another proposal being floated by the anti-South Africa bloc is that the OAU should agree to set up a fund with Arab money to assist countries to apply sanctions. According to a spokesman for the Pan-African Congress the main thrust of lobbying is towards countries like Senegal, the Ivory Coast and Malawi. What we are trying to do is persuade these states that the Soweto massacre has proved their policies wrong and they should join the bulk of Africa in confronting apartheid head on.
(The Guardian, 28 June 1976.)

The scale of unrest in 1976.

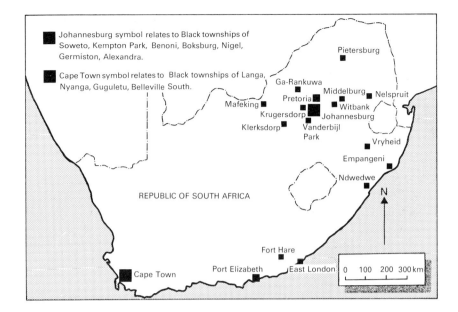

Johannesburg symbol relates to Black townships of Soweto, Kempton Park, Benoni, Boksburg, Nigel, Germiston, Alexandra.

Cape Town symbol relates to Black townships of Langa, Nyanga, Guguletu, Belleville South.

REPUBLIC OF SOUTH AFRICA

0 100 200 300 km

SOURCE 162 — The South African Government replies to the world

In the face of an American threat to impose sanctions Prime Minister Vorster said in August 1977 that the American government was embarking on a course that would lead to chaos and anarchy in South Africa. The only difference between American pressure and communist revolution was one of method — 'strangulation with finesse (style) instead of death by brute force'.

In September 1977, Mr Vorster called a General Election. Among the reasons he gave was that certain governments and world organisations were trying to meddle in South Africa's affairs. They had no right to say how the country should be governed. President Carter's meddling was a strong theme of the National Party election campaign. The National Party won 134 of the 165 seats in Parliament. The highest ever gained by any single party in South Africa.

('The Sanctions Handbook' by Roger Omond and Joseph Hanlon, Penguin Books, 1987.)

Questions

1. Using the statements from Kruger in Source 159 about Africans being 'Tame to the Gun', Brigadier Visser's comments about using 'sterner methods' and Sources 158 and 159, comment upon the methods used by the police in Soweto in June 1976.
2. In what ways does Source 159 contradict the statements in Sources 155 and 156? Can you account for this difference?
3. In Source 159 Kruger blamed the unrest on agitators. Who or what was he blaming? Is there any evidence which might confirm Kruger's accusations?
4. Using Source 158 and the map at the top of this page state what effect the shootings had on:
   a. The people of Soweto.
   b. Africans elsewhere in South Africa.
5. Was the unrest in 1976 different from that in South Africa following the Sharpeville Massacre in 1960?
6. What effect would the picture on page 89 have on world opinion?
7. What action could the world take to show its disapproval of South Africa? Were the measures effective?
8. What was Prime Minister Vorster accusing the United States of trying to do? Is there anything unusual about the accusation?
9. How was the election of 1977 white South Africa's response to the world?

The 1980s: Resistance and Reform

This chapter deals with the following topics:
1. The reforms introduced by the government in the 1980s.
2. The creation of the United Democratic Front.
3. New leaders for the 1980s: Desmond Tutu and Alan Boesak.
4. A new cycle of violence and repression.
5. The evidence that apartheid was being dismantled.

After reading this chapter and completing the exercises you will have:
1. Examined the reasons for the reform programme.
2. Looked at the aims of the UDF and the ideas of the new leaders.
3. Discovered the causes of the renewed unrest.
4. Examined the government's reaction to the unrest and the consequences of repression.

The worldwide criticism of South Africa at the time of the Soweto riots worried businessmen and some politicians. The new American President, Jimmy Carter, made human rights an issue and threatened to impose sanctions. There was a belief that some limited reforms would enable non-white South Africans to share in the country's increasing economic prosperity. They argued that improved living standards would make African workers more content and less willing to support those opposed to apartheid.

In 1979 the first reforms made black trade unions legal and gave them the right to negotiate with employers over pay and conditions. At the same time some apartheid laws, such as the Separate Amenities Act, were scrapped. These changes were described as cosmetic, because they only affected the surface. The Group Areas Act and the Homelands Policy remained. The government passed the running of black townships into the hands of black councillors. They argued that this was an important stage in meeting black demands for a democratic South Africa. The Township councils proved to be unpopular with the majority of residents. The councillors were seen as agents of the government, especially as they were to be responsible for collecting rents.

◀ Why did South Africa begin to introduce a series of reforms after 1976?

SOURCE 163 — The reforms

Solly Madlala is a resident of Soweto. Just after the riots in 1976 he had said that life in Soweto was bad and life hardly worth living. In 1980 some things had changed for the better.

Going to the Post Office before, we had to wait hours on end just because there were three whites, we being a hundred or more. Today all that has been eliminated and it satisfies me in such a way that what I used to do in two hours, today I'm doing it in about forty-five minutes. Without any commotion everybody is being

President and Mrs Botha.

served, like a person. Even we black people are being seen as people, living human beings, not like before.
('The White Tribe of Africa' by David Harrison, BBC Publications, 1985.)

In 1982 Prime Minister P. W. Botha announced important constitutional changes. Coloureds and Asians were to be given their own Parliament and would be represented in the government. The decision to share power caused a split in the National Party. More important was the reaction of non-white South Africans. The reforms did not include the Africans; they were to have no part in the government. Black community groups, coloured politicians and many members of the Asian community and many whites objected to the reforms. If there were to be reforms they demanded one person one vote. The coming together of so many different groups led eventually to the creation of a new force in South African politics: the United Democratic Front.

SOURCE 164 — P. W. Botha and the reforms
The alternative to sharing power is losing power. We face a threat from Black revolutionaries and without the Coloureds and the Indians as allies we might go under.

Those who want to abstain from voting and those who have been considering voting no — do you want to be in the company of the ANC? Decide for yourselves — I'm not accusing you.
(Extracts from speeches made by P. W. Botha to the National Party.)

SOURCE 165 — Alan Boesak on the elections
This is the same government who think they can play God in the lives of people. The same government who detain us without trial, who torture us in their jails and who ban those who stand up to speak for justice. Who throw our leaders on Robben Island or lock them up in Pollsmoor Prison. This is the government who want you to go out and vote.

You must be crazy to do that!
(Speech made on the eve of the elections, 20 August 1984.)

SOURCE 166 — The election results
Fewer than 18% of potential Coloured voters and 16% of potential Indian voters went to the polls. In the Cape the turn-out of voters was about 5%. One Coloured MP was elected with only 118 votes.
('The Apartheid Handbook', Roger Omond, Penguin Books, 1986.)

The first meeting of the UDF in Cape Town, formed to organise a boycott of the elections to the Coloured and Indian parliaments. The UDF has since become one of the most important opposition groups in South Africa. It has linked many different groups from a variety of backgrounds such as trade unions and community groups.

New Leaders: Alan Boesak and Desmond Tutu

The South African government's reaction to opposition leaders has been to arrest, ban and imprison them. Those not caught have been forced into exile. In the present unrest two South Africans have become worldwide figures and have remained at liberty. Desmond Tutu and Alan Boesak are both outspoken clergymen. Desmond Tutu is the Archbishop of Cape Town and the winner of the Nobel Peace Prize. Alan Boesak is one of the leaders of the United Democratic Front.

Alan Boesak, one of the founders of the UDF.

SOURCE 167 — Alan Boesak speaks

The Reforms

Change is unavoidable. It is just a question of how costly the government wants to make it. When we talk about change we mean fundamental reforms — the redistribution of land, wealth and political power. Cosmetic changes aren't acceptable to the blacks. The time that the people could be bought with petty concessions is past.

Township Violence

Government repression has led to unbelievable atrocities. In a Johannesburg township children have been shot in front of their homes. The unrest we see now is not going to be over in a couple of months like the Soweto uprising of 1976. People are no longer intimidated by guns.

The Future for South Africa

The only road to peace is the abolition of apartheid. We should work towards a National Convention where representatives of all the people of South Africa come together to scrap discrimination. President Botha must realise he could do things if he had the courage and the wisdom. He must realise that ethnic politics are dead. The cost of maintaining apartheid is tremendous, millions a

day. The whites may be afraid of the future, but at the UDF we tell them that our struggle is their struggle. We don't want the Afrikaners to go back to Holland. We want them here, but we also want them to know that this is not just their country.
(From an interview in a South African Magazine.)

SOURCE 168 — Desmond Tutu speaks

On Peaceful Protest and Change

It is a wonder that they still regard me as a leader. I've said to them let's see if we can change this system peacefully and I've not delivered the goods. In a meeting I was giving my usual line about peaceful change. After the meeting a boy of about twelve said 'Bishop do you believe what you are saying? Show me what you have gained with all your talk of peaceful change and I'll show you what we've gained with a few stones.' We've got a new breed of children and they believe they're going to die many of them — and the frightening thing is they don't care. In their view the only language that the government understands is violence.

Peaceful protest has become a virtual impossibility in our country. Passive resistance and non-violence presumes a certain minimum moral level. Gandhi knew there were people in England who would be morally outraged by the things that their troops were doing in India and would press for change. I'm not certain that in South Africa we have that certain moral level.

On Government Violence

The situation in South Africa is violent, and the primary violence is the violence of apartheid. It is the violence of forced removals, of detention without trial, of mysterious deaths in detention. Eight hundred children are picked up in Soweto, some as young as seven, and a lot of those children have to spend the night in cells. A boy of eleven is kept in cells for fifty-seven days. At a funeral a teenager has her teeth kicked out by the police, and our people are killed as if their deaths amounted to little more than the swatting of flies.

On Black Violence

The world is filled with people who support us and who want us to be free. And when they see that awful thing happen there (a necklace killing which was filmed and shown on news reports) many of them said — Uh-Uh — if these people can still do things like this maybe they are not yet ready for freedom.

Desmond Tutu.

Questions

1. Which laws have been repealed to make Solly Madlala's working life a little easier?
2. Source 164 outlines President Botha's attitude to reform. How did he persuade the whites to vote in favour of these reforms in a referendum in 1983?
3. What was Alan Boesak's opinion of the election? From Source 166, did many Africans agree with him?
4. In what ways are the views of Alan Boesak and Desmond Tutu on violence similar?
5. What do you think Alan Boesak means when he says that 'cosmetic changes aren't acceptable'?
6. What evidence is there to support Desmond Tutu's fear that peaceful protest is becoming more difficult?
7. Desmond Tutu's opinions on violence might upset some blacks as well as many whites. Why might this be so?

The 1980s: A Cycle of Violence

In August 1984, during the election campaign for the Indian and Coloured Parliament, the UDF urged people not to vote. The election campaign increased tension in South Africa. When Township Councils tried to increase rents in September there were violent protests in the Vaal Triangle, an area close to Johannesburg and Pretoria. Community groups organised rent strikes and by the end of the year the Councils were bankrupt, the councillors forced to leave and the army was sent in to restore order.

Before long protestors were being killed by police, and funerals became mass political demonstrations. A depressing cycle of violence became established. Demonstrators at funerals were killed and in turn their funerals led to further demonstrations. Unrest spread throughout black townships in South Africa.

In March 1985 at the African township of Langa, outside Uitenhage in the Eastern Cape, a funeral procession was halted by police who opened fire on the mourners. It was twenty-five years to the day that the Sharpeville massacre occurred. Insensitivity or police incompetence, the results were the same. This tragic sequence of events was seen by the rest of the world. In townships throughout South Africa the unrest became more ferocious.

SOURCE 169 — The Langa shootings

The crowd was on its way to a funeral in the township of Kwannoubile. The procession had been banned by a local magistrate but hundreds of mourners had boarded buses and taxis when they were intercepted by police. They proceeded on foot.

According to Louis Le Grange, Minister of Law, the crowd of between three and four thousand were armed with stones, sticks and petrol bombs and were heading to the white town of Uitenhage. Mr Le Grange said that the crowd advanced on and stoned a police detachment of nineteen men. The police warned them to disperse and then opened fire.
(The Guardian, 21 March 1985.)

SOURCE 170 — The Inquiry into the Langa shootings

During the course of the inquiry the following details emerged.

If the police had not been there there would have been no trouble. The whole thing was a peaceful march and there was no need for police action. The police had not followed basic instructions. No order to disperse was given and no tear gas was used. This is contrary to all instructions.
(Witness Helen Suzman, PFP Member of Parliament who visited Langa the day after to talk to people in Langa.)

His original statement said that he fired a warning shot after police and armoured vehicles were stoned by a black crowd and after the leader of the crowd produced a bottle. Rioters have frequently used petrol bombs.

He later said that he fired the warning shot before any stones were thrown: 'I wouldn't have fired a warning shot then because it would have been too late.'

Lt. Fouche said that he saw only one woman throw a stone before he gave the order to fire.

He also claimed that just two days before the shooting the police in Uitenhage had been given permission by Police Headquarters in Pretoria to use lethal weapons.
(Witness Lieutenant John Fouche, the Police Officer in command in Langa on 20 March.)

The 25th anniversary of Sharpeville — a cartoon by Gibbard which appeared in the 'Guardian'.

The inquiry also heard:

That tear gas, rubber bullets and bird shot had not been issued at Uitenhage since February.

Medical evidence presented showed that 17 out of 19 of the victims had been shot in the back.

Witnesses for the government wanted to point out that the wounds in the back were not always the fatal or the only wound.

Of those killed 9 were under 16. One of the youngest victims was Fundisu Wambif, 11 years old, who was killed by shotgun pellets.

The official death toll was 19, but community leaders have insisted that at least 43 were killed.

The funerals of those killed in the unrest often turned into political demonstrations. After the crowds of mourners came into conflict with the police, this set up a depressing cycle of funerals, demonstrations, shootings and yet more funerals.

The 1980s Black Opposition Groups

The government blamed the unrest on communists, agitators and the ANC, but the leaders of the ANC say that they were taken by surprise. As the unrest continued the ANC has become more involved. It is their intention to make the Townships ungovernable. A significant feature of the unrest is the part played by students and schoolchildren. In some townships groups of young activists have established an alternative authority. The Comrades have enforced boycotts, stay-at-homes and have punished people considered to be police informers.

As in 1976, children and young people have been at the forefront of street protests. The police and, since the State of Emergency, soldiers, have been sent into black Townships to try and stop the unrest. The presence of armed troops and armoured cars has itself provoked unrest. In 1985 and early 1986 the way the police dealt with unrest was shown by the world's press and television. The television images of violence did much to provoke worldwide criticism of the government. To counteract this, the government has imposed increasingly harsh restrictions on the media.

In June 1985 the government imposed a 'partial' State of Emergency. The order was applied in 36 areas where there had been unrest. The Emergency gave the police and the South African Defence Force even wider powers of arrest and detention. Journalists and newsmen were prevented from entering areas where the Emergency was in force.

SOURCE 171 — The ANC and the unrest

The unrest is well controlled, which is why it has been sustained since 1984. There has never been anything like it in the past. If it were not controlled it would have been snuffed out.
(Oliver Tambo President of the ANC.)

A state of civil war already exists, the battle lines are drawn. It is not a racist war, we are not fighting whites as whites, we are fighting a system.

The people are angry, they witness death in the cities of South Africa every day. ANC units are instructed to avoid indiscriminate bombing. But young people are losing relatives and friends. In the heat of the moment white civilians are attacked.
(Chris Hani, Deputy Military Commander of Umkhonto We Sizwe.)

SOURCE 172 — Black on Black violence — Crossroads squatter camp

Crossroads is a squatter camp on the outskirts of Cape Town. Few of the residents live there legally. In 1985 the government abandoned plans to forcibly move squatters to new locations at Cape Flats some 40 kilometres away. In June 1986 Crossroads erupted in violence as rival black groups fought.

We could not escape the huge pall of smoke that hung over Crossroads for much of our second visit. There, we were informed, black vigilantes, with active backing of the security forces, were attacking supporters of the UDF, including women and children, and setting fire to their shanties. Some thirty-three were killed and many more injured and upwards of 30,000 made homeless.

From what we heard and saw, there appeared to be a pattern of vigilante violence directed against blacks agitating for change. The violence is organised by those who have a stake in the 'system' and are being encouraged by the authorities.
('Mission to South Africa' The Report of the Commonwealth Group, Penguin Books, 1986.)

Violence flared up in Crossroads Squatter Camp in May 1986 when the 'Vigilantes', usually older residents who had an interest in the camp, attacked members of the UDF and other anti-apartheid groups. They were seen to be co-operating with the South African Defence Force, which frequently took no action against 'Vigilante' violence. Many were killed and large areas of the settlement were destroyed by fire. The government had been wanting to move illegal squatters in Crossroads for many years.

SOURCE 173 — Black-on-Black violence — The Government view

More than a third of the deaths and injuries in the unrest is the result of 'Black on Black' violence as radical activists have tried to intimidate and force law-abiding black communities into toeing their revolutionary line.

Statistics for the period September 1984 to May 1986 show that Black on Black violence claimed 448 lives. Another 761 people were killed during security force actions, most of these deaths resulting from security forces acting in self-defence.

('Southern Africa Facts Sheet', June 1986. Published by the South African Government.)

Police unrest report.

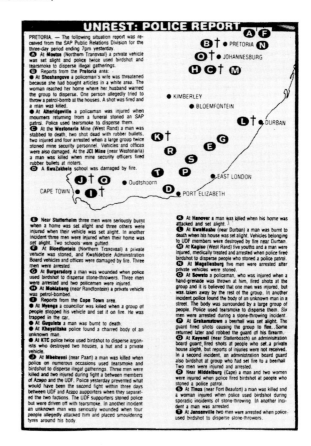

Government spokesmen attempted to play down the scale of the violence in the townships, which was directed against the police and army. Instead they concentrated on the 'black-on-black' incidents. They gave the impression that most of the unrest was the result of fighting between rival black groups.

SOURCE 174 — Winnie Mandela and Black-on-Black violence

This is now the right time to take your country. We shall use the same language the Boers are using against us. They only know one language — the language of the Kaspirs (armoured cars). We have no arms, we have stones, we have boxes of matches. With our necklaces we shall liberate this country.

(From a speech made in 1986.)

Questions

1. What was the original cause of unrest in September 1984? What is meant by the phrase a 'self-sustaining cycle of violence'?
2. In what ways was the government statement in Source 169 similar to those made in 1960 and 1976?
3. Either Louis Le Grange was badly informed or else he was trying to cover up for the police. How true is this statement based on the information available in Sources 169 and 170?
4. What point is the cartoonist trying to make on page 97.
5. Is there any truth to the claims made by Oliver Tambo in Source 171

6. Why should the government pay so much attention to Black-on-Black violence. How is this illustrated by the report at the foot of page 99.
7. Who do the government blame for Black-on-Black violence? From the evidence of Source 172 are the government blaming the right people?
8. The speech made by Winnie Mandela in Source 174 was widely reported in white South African papers and the other media. Can you explain why?

The 1980s New Opposition Groups

Chief Gatsha Butelezi, Chief Minister of the Kwa Zulu Homeland. While opposed to the UDF and the ANC he has refused to co-operate with the government. Kwa Zulu has been offered its independence like Transkei, but Buthelezi says he wants a united South Africa with 'one man one vote' as his eventual aim.

Black opposition to apartheid in South Africa is not united. Groups like AZAPO follow a line similar to the PAC of the 1960s or the Black Consciousness Movement of the 1970s. The UDF and the ANC have roughly similar views about the type of South Africa they would like to see after apartheid. There is one other group whose views and methods are not so clear. Inkatha is one such group. Its members belong to one tribal group, the Zulu, and are led by their Chief, Gatsha Buthelezi. As leader of six million Zulu his views are important. Buthelezi rejects the creation of a Zulu homeland, he is opposed to apartheid, but his methods have brought criticism from the UDF and the ANC who consider him to be a 'koiyoko' — a sell-out.

The other important groups in South Africa are the black trade unions. Their membership has grown considerably since the 1970s and they have considerable economic power. In November the Congress of South African Trades Unions (COSATU) was formed. Its aims were far more political than the Federation of South African Trade Unions (FOSATU). The combination of economic power in the ability to call strikes and a radical political outlook is seen as a threat. COSATU is still young and its influence is growing, especially amongst black miners; with half a million members it is an important voice.

SOURCE 175 — Chief Buthelezi speaks

Any system which disregards the rights of 72 per cent of South Africa's population is a fraud. But I don't seek upheavals. Blacks and whites need each other. There's room for negotiation and gradual progress. We and the majority of black South Africans reject the revolutionary violence proclaimed by the ANC. We reject the use of bombs. They will not topple the government, but kill and maim ordinary black citizens. The exiled prophets of violence are out of touch with the people in South Africa. The ANC is determined to make the country ungovernable through the employment of violence. The problem with that strategy is that it will make the country ungovernable for any future regime — black, white or mixed. Our liberation will be achieved through the give and take of compromise politics. If that makes me a puppet or a stooge in the eyes of the radicals, so be it.

SOURCE 176 — The programme of COSATU

We are living in urgent times and it is urgent to make it clear to the South African government, employers and society where the working people, united under the banner of COSATU, will stand.

It is important to realize that the political struggle is not only to remove the government. We must also eliminate unemployment and improve education and health facilities. The wealth of this society must be shared among all who work in this country.

We must meet with progressive political organisations. We have to work in co-operation with them on realistic campaigns. We must not shy away from them and pretend they do not exist.
(Cyril Ramaphosa, General Secretary of COSATU, speaking at the first meeting of COSATU in November 1985.)

The increasing unrest has affected the attitude of some whites in South Africa. Industrialists and businessmen, worried by the threat of sanctions abroad and industrial unrest at home, have taken matters into their own hands. In September 1985 Gavin Relly and a group of leading industrialists flew to Lusaka in Zambia for talks with ANC leaders. In July 1987 white Afrikaner politicians again met ANC leaders at Dakar in West Africa. Their aim was to find some common ground between the ANC and liberal white South Africans. There were calls for the whites to be charged with treason on their return to South Africa and two weeks after the meeting one of the organisers, a black trade unionist, was found murdered. Some whites who took part in the meeting were threatened with being hanged from the nearest tree.

SOURCE 177 — The ANC and the industrialists
They talked for six hours about the problems of violence, reconstruction, nationalisation and the country's economic future. The businessmen predictably asked about the threat of nationalisation which was included in the ANC's Freedom Charter. Tambo insisted that some corporations would have to be taken under state control. 'They represent tremendous wealth in the midst of unspeakable poverty.'
('Black and Gold', by Anthony Sampson, Hodder and Stoughton, 1987.)

COSATU rally. Cosatu is a new trade union movement and is a strong supporter of the UDF.

Questions
1. In what ways are the ideas and policies of Chief Buthelezi:
   a. similar, and
   b. different
   from those of the ANC?

2. Do you think that COSATU is just a trade union interested in improving the pay and working conditions of its members?

3. Does the rise of a movement like COSATU help to explain the events described in Source 177?

The 1980s: Is Apartheid Being Dismantled?

In response to the worldwide criticism, the South African Government claim that apartheid is being dismantled. The vote given to the Coloured and Indian communities ignored the majority African population. Nevertheless the Government point to the many apartheid laws which have been repealed. One of the first to go was the Separate Amenities Act, responsible for the rash of signs visible all over South Africa. The Morality Laws have been abolished, but, as Nelson Mandela once pointed out, it was not his ambition in life to marry a white woman. The disappearance of the Pass Laws was welcomed by all Africans as is the promised end to forced removals. The government still has a long way to go and many Africans do not believe that the government is willing to introduce real reforms. Until Africans see a real change in their lives they are not convinced by the government's claims.

Despite the claims that apartheid is an outdated idea, local authorities are still free to maintain separate facilities, as these beach signs in Natal show. By swimming on a 'whites only' beach, Allan Hendrickse, leader of the Labour Party in the Coloured Assembly, broke the law and angered President Botha.

SOURCE 178 — President Botha announces the end of Apartheid

Attempts are continuously being made to belittle each step forward and to brand all government initiatives as merely cosmetic. We have outgrown the outdated colonial system of paternalism as well as the outdated concept of apartheid. The government has become conscious of black aspirations and needs. The proposed programme for the coming session confirms our commitment to equal opportunities.

Among the most important matters are the following:

The involvement of Black communities in decision making.
A uniform identity document for all population groups.

Restoring South African citizenship to black persons who live in the Republic of South Africa but who lost their citizenship as a result of granting independence to Transkei, Bophutatswana, Venda and Ciskei.
(President Botha's Address at the Opening of Parliament, January 1986.)

SOURCE 179 — Reforming Apartheid

What has changed?
● Segregation in sport ended.
● De-segregation of numerous facilities — at the discretion of local authorities.
● Ending of ban on non-white businesses in town centres.
● Prohibition of Mixed Marriages Act repealed.
● Immorality Act repealed.
● Prohibition of Political Interference Act repealed, allowing political parties with multi-racial membership.
● Some job reservation laws ended.
● Trade Union rights given to non-white groups.
● Pass Laws scrapped.
● Influx Control Laws relaxed.
● Africans permitted to own property in African Townships.
● Improvements in educational opportunities for all.
('South African Facts Sheet', April 1986, Published by South African Government.)

103

SOURCE 180 — The Commonwealth and Apartheid.

We are sceptical of the intentions of the Government to dismantle completely apartheid in the sense that it is understood. Their actions up to this point do not justify any claim that apartheid is being dismantled. The essential pillars remain: the homelands policy, the Population Registration Act and the Group Areas Act. Not only do they remain but the 'homelands' policy is being further developed.

('Mission to South Africa' by the Commonwealth Eminent Persons Group, Penguin Books, 1986.)

◄ How would the following people respond to the claim that the reforms being introduced were just cosmetic:
  a. A supporter of the UDF?
  b. A member of the Afrikaner National Party?
◄ What law had Allan Hendrickse broken in Source 181? Does this throw any light on the claims that apartheid is being dismantled?

SOURCE 181 — The end of separate amenities?

In a humiliating backdown, the leader of South Africa's coloured representatives Mr Allan Hendrickse, apologised to President Botha yesterday for his defiant swim on a whites only beach.

In his apology, Mr Hendrikse said that his swim was not intended as an act of civil disobedience.

(The Guardian, 22 January 1987.)

The 1980s — The Government Reaction

The State of Emergency, which was introduced in 1985, was lifted in March of the following year. It had not succeeded in stopping unrest. In June 1986 anti-apartheid groups planned protest marches and stay-at-home strikes to commemorate the tenth anniversary of the Soweto uprising. In an effort to calm the situation the government imposed a second State of Emergency, which applied to the entire country. In December the government went even further by imposing severe limitations on press and television reporting. This affected South African media and foreign journalists working in South Africa.

Opposition to the reforms also came from many whites. They were concerned that the changes went too far and that the unrest was getting out of hand. White opposition showed itself in increased support for right wing groups.

SOURCE 182 — The 1985 state of emergency

In order to counter the organised campaign of violence the South African Government proclaimed a State of Emergency in 36 Districts on July 1985. The State of Emergency affected only 2% of the total surface area of South Africa. Government spokesmen pointed out that the partial state of emergency had been introduced to restore law and order, essential if political change and reform was to be proceeded with at the desired pace. A climate of violence is not conducive to reform.

('Southern Africa Factsheets', June 1986, published by the South African Government.)

The Government's action in respect of the present unrest has been largely successful. There has been a noticeable decline in incidents in certain areas and an improvement in the general climate. The situation is being monitored and the Government will not hesitate to counter any situation with even greater powers than we have used in the past. The South African Police and other security forces will fight those persons and organisations wishing to destroy our civilised way of life with everything in our power until they change their views or are destroyed.

(Louis le Grange, Minister of Law and Order, 18 February 1985.)

SOURCE 183 — The terms of the 1985 emergency

Under the Terms of the Emergency it was an offence to:
- Prepare, print, publish or possess a threatening document.
- Disclose the name or identity of anybody arrested under the emergency regulations before the name had been officially confirmed.
- Make statements calculated to subvert the government.
- Incite people to resist or oppose the government.
- Advise people to stay away from work or to dislocate industry.

The Police and Security Forces had the power to:
- Search people, premises and vehicles.
- Seal off any area to control entrance and departure.
- Close off any public or private place.
- Remove any person from a particular place.
- Order curfews during which people might be on the streets.
- Control or prohibit the distribution of news or comment on the emergency regulations or the conduct of any security officer.

('The Apartheid Handbook' by Roger Omond, Penguin Books, 1986.)

Police moving on a television crew. Television and the press have more and more restrictions placed on them under the State of Emergency and all news has to be approved by the government. Any journalist, whether from South Africa or abroad, faces severe penalties for breaking the rules on reporting scenes of unrest.

SOURCE 184 — The media and the unrest

Organisers of unrest soon learnt the publicity value of television and television crews were often given advance notice of the next 'spontaneous' outbreak of violence. David Braun of the *Johannesburg Star* said that a television journalist had been found paying black youngsters to burn their school books and a camera crew that had missed earlier action asked a crowd of blacks to re-enact a stone throwing scene. In another case shop owners reported that television crews had arrived in a peaceful street well before violence erupted.

In order to counter this situation, the Government decreed last November (1985) that local and foreign journalists could only film and record unrest if they had police permission. The impact was immediate and dramatic, the number of incidents of serious unrest declining by about 49% between October and November.

('Southern Africa Factsheets', June 1986, published by the South African Government.)

SOURCE 185 — What happened during the state of emergency

Numbers arrested 6733. (This does not include people arrested during incidents of unrest.)

Approximately 70% of those arrested had links with the UDF.

Between July and November 1985, 483 people were killed by the security forces.

A Port Elizabeth surgeon catalogued 153 cases of assault against detainees.

In Soweto 745 young persons were detained; in the Western Cape a boy of 10 was detained and a 12-year-old Soweto boy was arrested at 2.00 a.m.

Questions

1. In Source 182 the government spokesman uses phrases like:
   'partial state of emergency' and
   'affected only 2% of the surface area of the country.'
   What impression do these phrases give of the unrest?
2. Can you suggest why government spokesmen use such terms as those outlined in Question 1?
3. Sources 183 and 185 describe the powers and the activities of the security forces during the state of emergency. Do they confirm the comment by Louis le Grange that the authorities will do 'everything in their power' to deal with the unrest?
4. According to Source 184 what were the reasons for introducing restrictions on television crews and journalists? Might there be other reasons for banning journalists from areas of unrest?

The 1980s: The White Reaction

Since 1982 President Botha has had to face growing opposition from right-wing groups opposed to his reform programme. In 1982 Andries Treurnicht left the National Party with twenty-two other MPs to set up a new Conservative Party and, in a by-election held in 1983, won the seat from the National Party. Despite this, Botha was encouraged by the results of the 1983 referendum. Whites overwhelmingly voted in favour of the constitutional reforms. During the campaign Botha cleverly pointed out that anyone voting against the changes would be on the same side as the ANC.

As violence in the townships flared up more whites turned to extreme Afrikaner groups. The Afrikaner Resistance Movement (AWB) led by Eugène Terre Blanche was violently opposed to the reforms. Like the Ossewa Brandwag, the AWB saw itself as the protector of traditional Afrikaner ideas, and comparisons have been made between the AWB and the Nazis. Certainly the uniforms, the swastika-like symbol and the talk of a racially pure Afrikaner Volk have echoes in Hitler's Germany.

SOURCE 186 — White political parties

The National Party

This party has formed the government in South Africa since 1948 and was responsible for introducing apartheid. Under the reforms introduced by the National Party Coloured and Indian MPs have been given seats in Parliament. With the introduction of the 1986 State of Emergency and the setback in the 1987 elections the pace of reform appears to have slowed down.

The Conservative Party

Led by Andries Treurnicht, this party is opposed to the reform programme and wants a return to apartheid as it existed in the 1970s. After the 1987 election the Conservative Party is the official opposition party.

The Progressive Federal Party

The PFP has been described as the party of English liberals and the 'white conscience of South Africa'. Helen Suzman is perhaps the most outspoken and best known of opposition MPs. The PFP was the official opposition in Parliament until the 1987 election.

SOURCE 187 — The AWB

Throughout history, you and I have inherited the Afrikaner nation. All those before us were prepared to leave a will, a will they would write with their tears and their blood, one they would write in the starvation of children in concentration camps. They did this so that the outside world would know that here in darkest Africa is a small white nation with its own identity, its own language who exist as a nation.

We are the true freedom fighters. We fight for the honour and the self-respect and the sovereignty of our own nation where God is our King. In our veins flows the blood of Aryans, Christians and whites. Long live Afrikanerdom.
(Eugène Terre Blanche, speaking to an AWB meeting at the Voortrekker Monument in Pretoria in 1986.)

Eugène Terre Blanche of the Afrikaner Resistance Movement (AWB). At AWB rallies, uniforms, banners and the AWB symbol are much in evidence. There are many similarities with the pre-war Ossewa Brandwag, which had close links with the Nazis and European fascism.

SOURCE 188 — Andries Treurnicht

People who think that Mr Botha's reforms mean the end of the Afrikaner and white nationalism are making a big mistake. We will not allow them to create a mixture of people on the ruins of a white Christian culture and civilisation. We are not prepared to consider national suicide.

Some clergymen in their campaign against apartheid are actually campaigning for black domination and white surrender. I ask: How do certain ministers reconcile the cross of Christ worn around their neck with the communist flag under which they stand and preach.
(Andries Treurnicht, speaking to the Conservative Party Congress of the Transvaal in August 1985. 'Apartheid in Crisis', edited by M. Uhlig, Penguin Books, 1986.)

SOURCE 189 — The general election results May 1987

Party	Seats	
National Party	125	(120)
Conservative	20	(16)
PFP	19	(25)

Figures in brackets refer to seats held before the election.
(The Guardian, 8 May 1987.)

Questions

1. Using Sources 186, 187 and 188, can you identify which parties would suport President Botha's reform programme and which parties would oppose the reforms?

2. Who were the winners and losers in the May 1987 election?

Chapter 19

South Africa and the World

This chapter deals with the following topics:
1. South Africa's position in a changing continent.
2. South Africa's relations with her neighbours.
3. The world and South Africa.
4. Sanctions.

After reading this chapter and completing the exercises you will have:
1. Discovered how South Africa has reacted to the changes taking place in Africa.
2. Seen how the world has reacted to South Africa and South Africa's significance in the modern world.
3. Examined the arguments for and against sanctions.

When Malan became Prime Minister in 1948, South Africa was one of the very few independent countries in Africa. In the space of ten years great changes had begun to take place. Ghana became the first African colony to win freedom in 1957. The ending of colonial rule in Africa was sudden and in some cases bloody. For South Africans black and white there were important lessons. The ANC were encouraged by the rise of black nationalism. The Afrikaners thought that black rule would mean chaos.

African independence. In 1970 Mozambique, Angola and Rhodesia were white ruled states and allies of South Africa. By 1987 they had become black majority ruled states hostile to South Africa. (Rhodesia was renamed Zimbabwe.) Currently (1988) Namibia is still controlled by South Africa but agreement has been reached about granting independence as Cuban troops are withdrawn from Angola.

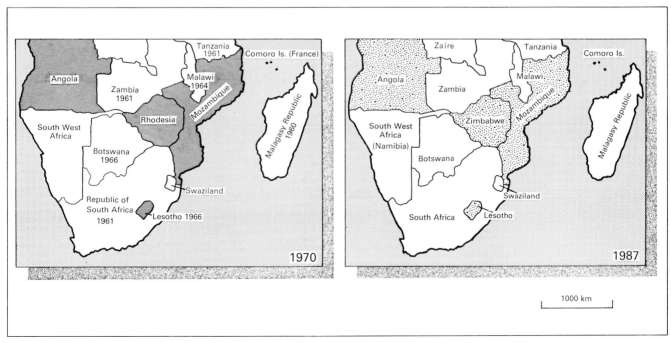

When the British Prime Minister, Harold Macmillan, visited South Africa in 1960 he spoke about the changes taking place in Africa and warned the whites of the consequences if they did nothing to meet the demands of their own people.

SOURCE 190 — Macmillan's 'Wind of Change' speech

As I have travelled round South Africa I have found everywhere concern with what is happening in Africa. I understand your anxiety. Since I left London the most striking impression I have formed is of the strength of African national consciousness.

The Wind of Change is blowing through the continent and, whether we like it or not, this growth of national consciousness is a political fact. We must accept it as a fact. That means we must come to terms with it. If we cannot do so we may imperil the peace of the world.

As a fellow member of the Commonwealth it is our desire to give South Africa our support and encouragement, but I hope you won't mind my saying frankly that there are some aspects of your policies which make it impossible for us to do this without being false to our own ideas about freedom.

◄ What was the 'Wind of Change' that Macmillan referred to in his speech?

A year later South Africa left the Commonwealth, preferring to go her own way rather than suffer continued criticism from the newly independent black nations. South Africa was not unduly worried about events elsewhere in Africa. Neighbours to the north had similar views to South Africa. Rhodesia declared her own independence in 1965 because she disagreed with Britain about black majority rule while Angola and Mozambique remained Portuguese colonies.

In 1974 South Africa's security was threatened; a revolution in Portugal resulted in Angola and Mozambique winning their independence almost overnight. To make matters worse, both Angola and Mozambique had Marxist governments. Five years later the white rule in Rhodesia had ended and Robert Mugabe became the leader of the new nation of Zimbabwe. In just 15 years South Africa's position in Africa had changed. South Africa was surrounded by hostile countries who not only criticised apartheid but supported and encouraged the ANC.

South Africa: A Regional Power

Despite being surrounded by hostile neighbours, South Africa has little to fear. It is by far the richest and most powerful nation in Africa. South Africa has a wealth of natural resources: gold, coal and in Namibia uranium. Manufacturing industry is well developed and the land is fertile and productive. During the colonial period transport and communication links were built to link South Africa with the rest of Southern Africa. The economies of the surrounding states are still tied to South Africa. Of equal importance is the size of the South African defence force; it is the largest and best equipped on the continent. South Africa can and does use its economic and military strength to threaten surrounding states.

SOURCE 191 — Economic dependence on South Africa

Country

	Lesotho	Sw'land	Botswana	Zimbabwe	Malawi	Zambia
A	RSA	RSA	RSA	RSA	RSA	UK
B	RSA	RSA	RSA	RSA	RSA	RSA
C	All	50%	Most	75%	33%	50%
D	100%	77%	21%	1%	0%	0%
E	Most	Some	Some	None	*	Little

A. Most important trading partner.
B. Country through which most imports pass.
C. Volume of country's trade passing through South Africa.
D. Percentage of electricity supplied by South Africa.
E. Food supplied by South Africa.
* Luxury Goods only. RSA, Republic of South Africa.
('Apartheid's Second Front', Joseph Hanlon, Penguin Books, 1986.)

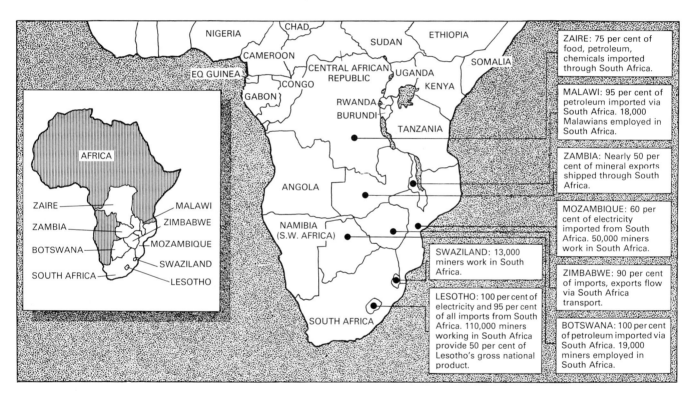

Southern Africa's dependence on South Africa.

SOURCE 192 — South African economic pressure

In 1981 South African Railways closed the border with Zimbabwe, stopping the export of meat, maize and tobacco. Oil was also stopped from going into Zimbabwe. The Zimbabwean government had to apply to the International Monetary Fund for a loan to prevent economic collapse.

In 1986 the border with Lesotho was effectively closed. The economic chaos led to the downfall of the government. The new leaders of Lesotho promised South Africa to stop the ANC operating in Lesotho.

South Africa is part of a customs agreement with Botswana, Lesotho and Swaziland which has tied the economies of these states to South Africa. Most of the advantages of this agreement lie with South Africa.

The nations of Southern Africa have tried to break the economic links, which make them so dependent on South Africa. In April 1980 the Southern African Development Co-ordinating Conference (SADCC) was set up. SADCC's aim is to link transport, trade and the economic development of Tanzania, Zimbabwe, Zambia, Botswana, Mozambique and Angola and later Lesotho, Swaziland and Malawi. The hope is that it will make the members of SADCC less reliant on South Africa.

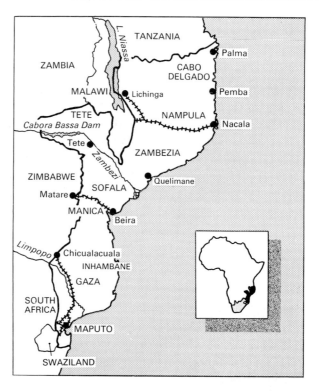

The importance of Mozambique in Southern Africa.

Questions

1. Look at the maps on page 109. How do they illustrate the idea of the 'Wind of Change'?
2. Have the changes which are shown on these maps affected the security of South Africa?
3. Using Source 191, state which country is:
   a. most reliant on South Africa?
   b. least reliant on South Africa?
   How would you use the information in the table to prove your answer?

4. Using Sources 191, 192 and the map on page 111 discuss how difficult it will be for the members of SADCC to make themselves less reliant on South Africa.

South Africa and Mozambique

Situated on the east coast of Africa, Mozambique occupies a very important position. Its ports of Maputo, Beira and Nacala and the railway lines which link the landlocked states could play a vital part in making countries like Zimbabwe, Zambia and Malawi less reliant on South Africa. The future of SADCC is dependent on the survival of Mozambique.

When Mozambique became an independent country in 1975 the FRELIMO government took over a country which was in a state of economic collapse. The problems facing Mozambique were worsened by continued fighting. FRELIMO found itself under attack from an organisation called the Mozambique

National Resistance. The MNR was organised and supplied by the security forces in Rhodesia. It was composed of former Portuguese soldiers, prisoners and former FRELIMO troops who were dissatisfied with the new government. The MNR was created to disrupt Mozambique by destroying economic targets, attacking road and rail links and terrorising the people.

When Black majority rule was established in Rhodesia in 1980 the South African Defence Force began to supply and equip the MNR. In 1982 the attacks on Mozambique started with even greater ferocity. A drought in much of Mozambique in 1983 led to widespread crop failure and added to the misery and 100,000 people are thought to have died. This series of disasters forced the Mozambique government to come to an agreement with South Africa. In March 1984 Samora Machel and P. W. Botha signed the Nkomati Accord. In return for a South African promise to stop supporting the MNR, Mozambique agreed to close ANC military bases in Mozambique and also to allow South African industry to invest in Mozambique. The agreement was criticised by some black African states but, as Samora Machel pointed out, the country was on the verge of collapse and had no choice.

SOURCE 193 — The MNR and the South African connection

Evidence for links between the South African Defence Force and the MNR are illustrated by captured documents from an MNR base in the Gorongosa Mountains. These show:

1. In February and March 1984 the MNR received arms and other supplies from South Africa on no fewer than 25 occasions.
2. South African instructions to the MNR telling them to concentrate their attacks near the capital Maputo and on road and rail links and power lines.
3. In July 1984 MNR leaders had met with the head of the South African Defence Force, General Viljoen, Pik Botha, Foreign Minister and Magnus Malan, Defence Minister.
4. In 1985, Deputy Foreign Minister Louis Nel illegally landed at the MNR base inside Mozambique for talks with the MNR leaders.

SOURCE 194 — The death of Samora Machel

In October 1986 the President of Mozambique was killed when his aircraft crashed into a hillside just inside South Africa close to the Mozambique border.

The Mozambican leadership announced President Samora Machel's death last night saying that the plane in which the President died 'crashed in circumstances which are not yet clarified'. Senior Mozambique officials flew to the crash site in a remote corner of South Africa but there was no immediate word of the cause.

Leaders of the six frontline states met in Maputo and declared that Samora Machel fell victim to apartheid. They noted that threats were made in the days before the crash and Pretoria had directed their menaces against Mr Machel. South Africa's Defence Minister, Magnus Malan, warned neighbouring countries to stop the vicious accusations.
(Reports from the Guardian, 21, 30, 31 October 1986.)

Samora Machel, President of Mozambique, welcomes Oliver Tambo, President of the ANC, to a meeting of the Front Line States.

◀ What problems have faced Mozambique since independence?

South Africa and Namibia

Namibia was first occupied by Europeans in the 1880s when it became the German colony of South West Africa. South African troops took over the colony in 1915 and after the First World War South Africa was meant to rule the country on behalf of the League of Nations and to look after the interests of the population.

Large areas of Namibia are desert and it has a small population. The land has valuable natural resources; diamonds are mined on the coast and one of the largest open-cast uranium mines in the world is in Namibia. Uranium is important as a fuel for nuclear power and for the manufacture of atomic weapons.

The United Nations became responsible for Namibia after 1945. The UN claimed that Namibia was a Trust Territory and that South Africa had at some time to prepare Namibia for independence. The South African government held a different view. With the end of the League of Nations, South Africa alone was responsible for Namibia and claimed that the UN had no claim to the land. After the 1948 elections the South African government divided Namibia into constituencies and it sent white MPs to the South African Parliament. South Africa was treating Namibia as part of South Africa. In 1966 the UN told South Africa to give Namibia its independence; South Africa refused and said that Namibia had nothing to do with the UN.

The introduction of apartheid laws in Namibia and the refusal to consider independence gave support to SWAPO — the South West Africa People's Organisation. SWAPO began a guerilla war against South Africa in 1966, which continues to this day. The guerilla war took a different turn when Angola was granted its independence in 1974 and a left-wing government took power with support from Cuban troops and Russian advisers. SWAPO has bases in Angola and the South African Defence Force have illegally invaded Angola several times, supposedly to destroy SWAPO camps. The war against SWAPO and the raids into Angola have proved expensive. Many South African soldiers have been killed and the government spends millions of Rand every year in Namibia. The South Africans are looking for a solution to their problems in Namibia and are trying to link independence to the removal of Cuban soldiers from Angola.

SOURCE 195 — The United Nations and Namibia
The General Assembly confirmed:
i.   that the people of South West Africa had the right to freedom and independence.
ii. that South Africa had failed under the League of Nations Mandate to ensure the well-being of the people.
iii. that South Africa had no right to administer the territory and South West Africa came under the direct responsibility of the United Nations.
(UN Resolution 2145 27 October 1966.)

SOURCE 196 — The aims of SWAPO
The tasks before SWAPO are:
1. The winning of independence for the people of Namibia by all possible means and the establishment of a people's government.

2. To organise the Namibian people so that they can participate in the liberation struggle. SWAPO believes that armed resistance to the South African occupation is the only effective means left to achieve liberation in Namibia.

SOURCE 197 — The South African Government and Namibia
As far as South West Africa is concerned, the Republic of South Africa remains prepared to implement the UN resolutions, provided agreement can be reached on Cuban withdrawal from Angola. Only then will the Republic of South Africa reduce its troops in terms of the agreed arrangements. In this area, lasting peace and freedom can only prevail if terrorism gives way to negotiation.
(President P. W. Botha's speech to Parliament, 31 January 1986.)

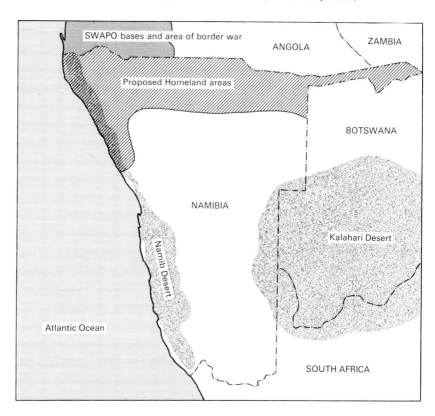

Namibia and neighbouring countries.

Questions

1. Using the map on page 112, can you say why Mozambique is important for the economic development of the members of SADCC? Can this help to explain why South Africa is interested in de-stabilising Mozambique?

2. What was the Nkomati Accord? From Source 193 can you say how effective the agreement has been?

3. Is there any evidence in Source 193 to suggest that the South African government was sincere in its desire to help Mozambique? (The dates of events are important here.)

4. Does the map on page 112 explain anything about South Africa's attitude to Mozambique? Is there any link between the map and Source 194?

5. In what ways is South Africa defying the world by its presence in Namibia?

6. Is there any evidence in the sources which explains why South Africa is reluctant to give Namibia its independence? Might there other reasons why South Africa wants to hold on to Namibia?

7. What is SWAPO and can you explain why it is fighting a guerilla war in Namibia?

Sanctions

Whenever politicians discuss South Africa, one issue seems to dominate the talks: sanctions. These are measures which countries can take against another either to show that they don't approve of that country or to try and force the country to change its ways.

There have been calls to impose sanctions against South Africa since the 1960s. One sanction is the boycott. The Commonwealth Prime Ministers signed the Gleneagles Agreement in 1977, which committed Commonwealth members to discourage all sporting links with South Africa and, since the 1960s, South Africa has been banned from the Olympic Games. The United Nations has imposed a 'Cultural Boycott' of South Africa. Actors, musicians and artists are forbidden to perform in South Africa. Such sanctions show that the world is opposed to apartheid, but they only cause inconvenience. Economic sanctions, which are now being called for, are meant to damage South African trade and industry and force the government to abolish apartheid.

SOURCE 198 — Basil D'Oliviera and the sport boycott

Basil D'Oliviera had gone to live in England because as a coloured man he wasn't allowed to play in the official leagues in South Africa. In England he had succeeded brilliantly in county cricket and had played for England against Australia, New Zealand, the West Indies and Pakistan.

Vorster's problem was that if he allowed D'Oliviera to tour South Africa with the England team it would anger right-wingers and make a mockery of apartheid. If he scored well against South Africa it would emphasise the injustice which prevented him from playing for his own country.

Eventually Vorster announced to the cheers of the National Party that D'Oliviera wouldn't be allowed in.

The result of the D'Oliviera ban and cancellation of the cricket tour was that it boosted the campaign against South Africa in world sport.
('Asking For Trouble' by Donald Woods, Penguin Books, 1980.)

SOURCE 199 — The cultural boycott

Johnny Clegg is an English born white singer who lives in South Africa where he has led two remarkable multi-racial bands that have battled against apartheid. Later this month, when the controversial Paul Simon tour is over, Clegg plans to return to Britain — if the Musicians Union will let him.

Clegg and his band could suffer more from the boycott than Paul Simon. Simon managed to bring South Africans to Britain because they had cleverly been signed up by the American Federation of Musicians. British born Clegg is a member of the Musicians Union but the Musicians Union says his residency in South Africa is incompatible with membership of the Union and that as part of the Cultural Boycott the Musicians Union normally opposes South African visits.
(Article by Robin Denselow in the *Guardian* 10 April 1987.)

SOURCE 200 — Black South Africa on sanctions

Sanctions are not to be seen as a way of reforming South Africa, nor just as a gesture of disapproval. Sanctions are a weapon that the international community can and must use against the racist régime.

Sanctions will not in themselves bring down the apartheid system. They are an important complement to the struggle of the South African people. The effect of sanctions will be to limit the duration of the war that is now raging in South Africa.
(Oliver Tambo, President of the ANC.)

Sanctions which will do more harm to the oppressed than the oppressors are madness. In the current economic crisis black people already bear the brunt of the hardship. More black suffering as a result of sanctions will not force the régime into accepting change. Black workers are not calling for measures which would bash the victims of apartheid.
(Chief Gatsha Buthelezi, Chief Minister of Kwa-Zulu.)

Many groups are now arguing against sanctions. I find it very interesting that for many years none of these groups has been concerned with the welfare of the blacks, yet now they are screaming and shouting about how the welfare of blacks will decline if sanctions are applied.
(Billy Nair, UDF Leader in Natal.)

The argument that blacks would be hurt by sanctions is all idle talk. We are suffering already from rampant poverty, disease and massive unemployment and a little suffering added to our burden won't make much difference. It is striking that this argument is pushed by those who enjoy privileged positions at work and in the community. It comes from those who have a stake in the scheme of things.
(Greg Malebo, member of General and Allied Workers Union.)

DON'T BUY SOUTH AFRICAN GOODS

DON'T BUY APARTHEID

This is the message coming loud and clear from black South Africans and Namibians. They are appealing to people all over the world to **boycott the products of apartheid.**

What is apartheid? It is the unique system of racial tyranny practised in South Africa. And the racist regime in South Africa has exported this evil system to Namibia which South Africa illegally occupies in defiance of international law.

Apartheid means power, privilege and wealth for the white minority. It means poverty, humiliation and exploitation for the black majority. Above all it means that the black majority are denied all fundamental political and human rights in their own country.

But why the boycott? Most importantly because black leaders in South Africa and Namibia have repeatedly called for the boycott. The isolation of apartheid South Africa is the most practical non-violent way for the international community to support their struggle for freedom. By boycotting South African and Namibian products, we are denying the apartheid regime much needed foreign exchange which it needs to arm and fuel the apartheid war machine.

Won't the boycott hurt blacks most? NO! It will above all hit the profits of those who benefit from apartheid. But blacks accept it may mean some sacrifice. Today black South Africans themselves are organising boycotts. They see the boycott as one of the weapons in their struggle for freedom.

But isn't apartheid being phased out? NO! There is much talk of 'reform' but there has been no fundamental change in the system of apartheid which is being enforced more and more brutally. Even the minor 'reforms' about which there is so much talk are the result of resistance inside South Africa and international pressure.

But will the boycott work? YES! It is working. There is widespread support for the boycott and a growing number of retail chains have banned South African and Namibian products or begun looking for alternatives. But the pressure must be kept up.

- -

☐ I want to help the fight against apartheid. My donation is for £................
☐ I would like information about how I can campaign against apartheid
☐ I would like to join the AAM (£9.00 waged, £5.50 students and apprentices, £3.50 unwaged, £12 joint membership)

Name . . . .
Address . . . .
. . . .

Please return to: Anti-Apartheid Movement, 13 Mandela Street, London NW1 0DW. Tel 01-387 7966.

The issue of sanctions divides opinion throughout the world as these posters show.

The issue of sanctions not only divides opinion in South Africa. It is an important world issue. The leaders of the Front Line States in Southern Africa stand to lose most if sanctions are imposed, simply because their economies are so dependent on South Africa. Despite this, they speak out loudest in favour of sanctions. They are willing to suffer the hardships if sanctions will help to speed up the end of apartheid. In the Western World two leaders have stood out in their opposition to apartheid — Margaret Thatcher the British Prime Minister and Ronald Reagan the President of the United States. At the 1986 Commonwealth Conference the leaders met to discuss the Report of the Eminent Persons Group which had visited South Africa between February and May 1986. Their report doubted the sincerity of the South African government's promise of reforms and saw little evidence that apartheid was being dismantled. It recommended that further sanctions be imposed, as had been agreed the previous year.

SOURCE 201 — Commonwealth Leaders and sanctions

I have to tell you, ladies and gentlemen, that I do not think comprehensive economic sanctions which would stop all trade with South Africa, would help to bring about change. I think it would lead to resistance to change and much more violence and bloodshed.
(Mrs Thatcher.)

Mrs Thatcher cut a very pathetic picture, a very pathetic picture indeed at the summit.
(Kenneth Kaunda, Prime Minister of Zambia.)

Britain has chosen the path of supporting apartheid.
(Robert Mugabe, Prime Minister of Zimbabwe.)

Really it's 48 to 1 and on any balance of probability it's more likely that the 48 are right.
(Robert Hawke, Prime Minister of Australia.)

SOURCE 202 — The 1985 Commonwealth Accord on South Africa

We consider South Africa's continuing refusal to dismantle apartheid and its aggression against its neighbours constitutes a serious challenge to the Commonwealth. We consider that the situation calls for urgent practical steps.

For our part, we have reached an agreement on a common programme of action. We commend to other governments the adoption of further economic measures against South Africa:
1. A ban on all new government loans to South Africa.
2. A ban on the import of Krugerrands.
3. No government funding for trade missions to South Africa.
4. A ban on the export of computer equipment capable of use by the South African military, police or security forces.
5. A ban on the sale and export of oil to South Africa.

Questions

1. What are sanctions? What different forms can they take?
2. What do the following people hope that sanctions will achieve:
   a. A member of the ANC?
   b. A foreign politician opposed to apartheid?
3. Why are the following people opposed to sanctions:
   a. Chief Buthelezi?
   b. President Botha?
4. What do the posters on page 117 reveal about attitudes to sanctions in Britain?
5. What are the arguments for and against imposing sanctions on South Africa?

The Strategic Importance of South Africa

Until the opening of the Suez Canal South Africa was a strategic part of the British Empire helping to protect the sea route to India and the Empire in the East. In the late 20th century does South Africa still occupy a strategically important position in the world?

We have seen how Western politicians are reluctant to impose strict sanctions against South Africa. They argue that sanctions will cause unemployment and hardship to the Africans in South Africa. However, sanctions have been applied in recent years against Poland, Libya and most recently in Panama. There doesn't seem to be too much concern about causing hardship to innocent Poles, Libyans or Panamanians. Might the reluctance of the West to impose sanctions be related to wider strategic issues?

Today South African politicians talk about the Third World War already having started in Southern Africa. They say that the nation is facing a 'total onslaught' from the Soviet Union which is seeking to establish Communist control in the whole of Southern Africa.

SOURCE 203 — The total onslaught
Describing the problems, Lt. General J. R. Dutton of the South African Defence Force said:
South Africa is facing a 'Total Onslaught'. Any conflict in Southern Africa is more or less directly related to the East-West conflict. The Soviet Union is waging a total war against South Africa using military, political, economic and cultural means. There can be no distinction between events outside and inside South Africa or military and non-military threats. Even labour strikes could be seen as 'guerilla actions'.
('Brutal Force', by Gavin Cawthra, IDAF Publications, 1986.

SOURCE 204 — South Africa and the Russian threat
The South African Government was encouraged that President Reagan saw the problems of the region in terms of east-west relations. South Africa's suspicion of the Soviet Union bordered on paranoia, so the new American Government's tough line towards Moscow was greeted in South Africa. White South Africans hoped that they would finally be regarded as an important part of the defence of the West.
('Apartheid In Crisis', edited by Mark Uhlig, Penguin Books, 1986.)

SOURCE 205 — The South African Defence Force
The SADF is the strongest in Africa, according to the International Institute for Strategic Studies. Under full mobilization 400,000 people could be called up — a figure supported by the military correspondent of the Cape Times. The IISS report said that South Africa had 250 tanks, 1,400 armoured cars, 500 armoured personnel carriers, 1,200 infantry combat vehicles, 313 combat aircraft, at least 10 combat helicopters and 80 other helicopters.
('The Apartheid Handbook', Roger Omond, Penguin Books, 1986.)

SOURCE 206 — Strategic minerals

For five types of minerals South Africa is the world's first or second producer and supplies at least one third of the Western world's consumption. These are manganese, vanadium, chromium, platinum and gold. The first three are essential to the steel industry, while platinum is vital for oil refining. Thus these are strategic minerals, and it is sometimes claimed that the loss of South African supplies would have catastrophic consequences for Western industry and military capability. Especially as the Soviet Union is often the next largest producer.

('The Sanctions Handbook', by Joseph Hanlon and Roger Omond, Penguin Books, 1987.)

SOURCE 207 — Margaret Thatcher and sanctions

To me it is absolutely absurd that people should be prepared to put increasing power into the hands of the Soviet Union on the grounds that they disapprove of apartheid in South Africa. If sanctions pushed up mineral prices that would have a fantastic effect on the economy of the Soviet Union.

('The Sanctions Handbook', by Joseph Hanlon and Roger Omond, Penguin Books, 1987.)

SOURCE 208 — President Reagan and South Africa

South Africa is one of the most vital regions in the world. Around the Cape of Good Hope passes the oil of the Persian Gulf — indispensable to the economies of the West. South Africa is a source of many vital minerals for which the West has no other secure source of supply. The Soviet Union knew the stakes: it had installed a Communist régime in Angola using Cuban troops. If the rising hostility in Southern Africa explodes, the Soviet Union will be the main beneficiary. And the critical ocean corridor of South Africa, and the strategic minerals of the region would be at risk.

('The Sanctions Handbook', by Joseph Hanlon and Roger Omond, Penguin Books, 1987.)

Questions

1. What evidence do you think a South African politician might use to justify the idea of a 'total onslaught'?

2. From Source 204 do you think the South African Government welcomed the election of Ronald Reagan in 1980?

3. Could the idea of a 'total onslaught' be in any way related to the information in Source 205? Knowing what you do of South Africa's neighbours, is it possible to believe the idea of a communist threat to the whole of Southern Africa?

4. How might Sources 206, 207 and 208 explain the reluctance of Western leaders to impose sanctions on South Africa?

Index

Glossary

Africanism
The policy of the Pan African Congress whose main idea is Africa for the Africans.

African National Congress
The ANC has been the largest and most influential group campaigning against apartheid. It is non-racial and its aim is a South Africa where black and white are equal. It was banned in 1960 following the Sharpeville Massacre.

Afrikaner
The largest white group in South Africa. The Afrikaners are the descendants of the original Dutch settlers.

Afrikaans
The language of the Afrikaner. While it is mostly Dutch, over a period of 300 years it has developed into a separate language.

Anglo-Boer War 1899-1902
The war between the Boer Republics of Transvaal and the Orange Free State and the British Provinces of the Cape and Natal. The main issue of the war was the continued independent existence of the Boer Republics.

AWB
The Afrikaner Resistance Movement. Led by Eugène Terre Blanche, the AWB has been described as a Nazi organisation. Its emblem is a three-armed hooked cross similar to the swastika. The AWB is violently opposed to the reforms of the National Party and sees itself as the protector of traditional Afrikaner ideas.

Apartheid
An Afrikaans word which means 'apartness'. The word was first used by the National Party in 1948 to describe the policy of segregation and discrimination against the non-European population of South Africa.

Assegai
A short stabbing spear which became the favoured weapon of the Zulu Impis during the 19th century.

Asians
The smallest of the four main population groups. The Asian population originally came from India and was employed to build the railways and work on the agricultural plantations of Natal.

Banning Order
An unusual punishment which may be imposed under the Internal Security Act. A Banned Person does not have to commit any criminal offence, yet the Minister of Law and Order has the power to ban someone to their house and forbid them to meet with more than one person at a time.

Bantu
The correct way to use this word is when describing a particular language grouping in Southern Africa. The National Party use the word to refer to any black South African.

Bantustan
These were the areas set aside as the tribal Homelands for South Africa's black population.

Biko, Stephen (1946-1977)
Born in the Eastern Cape. He went to University as a medical student but soon became involved in black politics. He was an active member of the National Union of South African Students but as his ideas developed he saw the need for black organisations to represent the views of black South Africans. He was a founder member of SASO, the South African Students Organisation. These ideas developed into the Black Consciousness Movement. In 1973 Biko was banned but he still managed to play an important part in the development of the Black Consciousness Movement. In 1977 he was arrested for breaking his banning order. While he was in police custody he sustained severe head injuries and died.

Black Consciousness

The Black Consciousness movement played an important part in the unrest of the mid-1970s. Black Consciousness taught black Africans that if they had pride in themselves they would be able to win their own freedom. The Black Consciousness movement was well supported by students and increased its following by creating self-help community groups.

Blood River

Site of a battle between the Trekkers and the Zulu on 16 December 1838. Despite being heavily outnumbered the Trekkers defeated the Zulu. The battle is remembered every year by the Afrikaners as one of the most important events in their history.

Boesak, Allan (1946-   )

Clergyman from Cape Town and one of the leaders of the United Democratic Front. With Archbishop Tutu, Allan Boesak is one of the most outspoken critics of apartheid. Because of his high profile the South African government has so far been unable to silence him.

Boer

An Afrikaans word which simply means farmer. In the 19th century it was applied to all Dutch-speaking South Africans almost as a term of abuse.

Bophuthatswana

One of the independent homelands created by the South African government. Bophuthatswana is the homeland of the Tswana. South Africa claims it has given the homeland its independence, but this is recognised by no other country. Bophuthatswana is unusual in that it is a series of 'islands' in the north west of the Transvaal.

Botha, Louis (1862-1919)

Botha was commander of the Boer armies in the Anglo-Boer War and was one of the men who signed the Treaty of Veeriniging in 1902. He became Prime Minister of the Transvaal in 1907 and was the first Prime Minister of the Union of South Africa. Through the South Africa Party, which he created, he hoped to heal the divisions caused by the Boer War. He supported Britain in the First World War and helped to organise the Campaigns against German Colonies in Southern Africa. He was criticised by more extreme Afrikaner Nationalists for being pro-British.

Botha, Pik (1932-   )

Present day Foreign Minister of South Africa.

Botha, P. W. (1916-   )

Leader of the National Party in the Transvaal and Minister of Defence. He became Prime Minister in 1978 and began to introduce a series of reforms. Under the new constitution he became President in 1984. His reforms have been criticised by right-wing Afrikaners.

Broederbond

A cultural society established in 1919 to promote Afrikaner ideas. It has become a secret society for the élite of South Africa's Afrikaner population. Every Prime Minister has been a member of the Broederbond.

Buthelezi, Chief Gatsha (1928-   )

Leader of South Africa's Zulu population and the homeland of KwaZulu in Natal. Buthelezi is a moderate politician who is opposed to sanctions and the ideas of the United Democratic Front. His followers belong to Inkatha, almost a Zulu political party.

Cape Province

One of the four regions of South Africa. It has a reputation of being more liberal and this may be because of the larger English-speaking population.

Cetswayo

Leader of the Zulus at the end of the 19th century. Under his leadership the Zulu fought unsuccessfully to stop a British invasion of Zulu lands. After he was captured Zulu lands became part of Natal.

Coloureds

People of mixed race, the largest numbers of coloured people live in the Cape. Under the British administration some coloured people were given the vote, but this right was later removed by the National Party.

Conservative Party

The constitutional reforms proposed by P. W. Botha angered right-wing Nationalists who were opposed to change. In 1984 Dr Andries Treurnicht left the National Party to form the Conservative Party. In the May 1987 election the Conservatives became the second largest party in the South African parliament. In recent by-elections support for the Conservative Party has grown considerably, showing that many Afrikaners are unhappy with the reforms.

COASAS

Confederation of South African Students, a black students' organisation which was set up in the 1970s as part of the Black Consciousness movement.

COSATU

Confederation of South African Trade Unions. COSATU is a grouping of black trade unions and was founded in 1985. It is more political than the older Federation of South African Trade Unions FOSATU. The General Secretary of COSATU, Cyril Ramaphosa, threatened the government with industrial action if apartheid was not reformed. COSATU is an important member of the United Democratic Front.

Crossroads

A large squatter camp on the outskirts of Cape Town. Africans who have not the legal right to live in urban areas or Africans who want to be with their families have moved to Crossroads without official permission. Several times the government has tried to demolish the camp and force the population to move to an official township. In 1986 unrest broke out in Crossroads when older residents clashed with supporters of the UDF.

Dingaan
Zulu chief in the 1830s. At the time of the Great Trek Piet Retief and others met with Dingaan to sign a Treaty. In Dingaan's kraal Retief and the other Trekkers were massacred. The massacre was avenged at the Battle of Blood River.

Dutch Reformed Church
The church of the Afrikaner. Many of the religious ideas of the Church were used to justify apartheid and the treatment of non-white South Africans.

Eminent Persons Group (EPG)
As a result of the 1985 Commonwealth Prime Ministers' Conference politicians from several Commonwealth countries visited South Africa to see if apartheid was being reformed and to suggest ways in which peaceful change could be brought about.

FOSATU
The Federation of South African Trade Unions. This grouping of different trade unions was formed in the 1970s. It is less radical than COSATU and committed to more traditional trade union activities.

Freedom Charter
In 1955 groups from all over South Africa met at Kliptown to agree upon a programme for the future government of South Africa. Its main aim was for the end of apartheid and the creation of a South Africa where all South Africans were equal. The Freedom Charter is still the programme of the ANC.

FRELIMO
Frelimo was originally a liberation movement which was fighting against the Portuguese authorities in Mozambique. In 1975 after the collapse of the Portuguese Empire Frelimo formed the new government of Mozambique.

Great Trek
This was the movement of Afrikaners out of British-controlled Cape Colony in 1836. Their aim was to set up an independent homeland where they would be free to live their traditional way of life away from British control.

Group Areas Act
This is one of the most important apartheid laws which was passed in 1950. The Act stated where the different racial groups could live in South Africa. It set up strictly segregated residential areas and any people living in the wrong area could be forcibly removed to the 'correct' area.

Hertzog, Barrie (1866-1942)
Another Boer military leader who became an important figure in the Union of South Africa. He was opposed to South Africa's entry into the First World War and broke away from the Government to form the National Party. In the Depression years following the First World War he entered into a coalition with Smuts. This lasted until 1939 when the Second World War began. He left the government again and joined Malan's Purified National Party.

Homelands
This is the term used today to describe the self-governing or semi-independent tribal areas (see Bantustans).

Hottentots
The original inhabitants of the Cape: this was a name given to them by the Dutch settlers. They called themselves the Khoikhoi.

Huguenots
French Protestants who left France to escape persecution in the 1680s. The language and traditions of the Huguenots have helped to make the Afrikaner culture and the Afrikaans language.

Inkatha
A Zulu cultural organisation whose leader is Chief Gatsha Buthelezi. Inkatha is more like a political party and claims to be the largest black organisation in South Africa. In Natal, where Inkatha is most powerful, there have been violent clashes between the UDF and Inkatha.

Internal Security Act
This law 'tidied up' the various laws which were used to put down protests. It replaced the Suppression of the Communism Act and the Terrorism Act. It gives the police and Security Forces tremendous powers to arrest detain and ban any opponents of apartheid.

Isandhlwana
This was the opening battle of the Zulu War of 1879. A force of British troops were caught ill prepared and 1800 soldiers died. It was the last time that any African army inflicted such a serious defeat on a European army.

Jameson, Leander Starr (1853-1917)
Jameson began his career in Kimberley working as a doctor; he was later employed by Cecil Rhodes' British South Africa Company. He led the failed raid into the Transvaal in 1895 which was meant to signal the beginning of an uprising against the government of the Transvaal. The Raid worsened relations between the Boer Republics and the British and was an important cause of the Anglo-Boer War.

Kaffir
An insulting term used by the Dutch to refer to the Xhosa people of the Eastern Cape. It was also used to describe a series of frontier wars with the Xhosa during the 19th century.

Khoi-Khoi and Khoisan
The native African people of the Cape. The Khoi-khoi were pastoral farmers, the Khoisan nomadic hunters.

Kruger, Paul
Leader of the Transvaal in the late 19th century. His determination to preserve the independence of Transvaal was one factor which led to the Anglo-Boer War.

Location
An African residential area.

Luthuli, Chief Albert (1898?-1967)

Clergyman, teacher and minor Zulu chief. Became a member of the Natives Representation Council but was dismissed when he used the meetings to complain about apartheid. He became leader of the ANC and was well-known outside South Africa. He was a defendant in the Treason Trial and spent the final years of his life as a banned person. He firmly clung to his ideas of non-violent protest.

Malan, Daniel (1874-1959)

A Transvaal journalist who opposed the growing influence of the Engish in South Africa. His newspaper did much to highlight the problem of the Poor Whites. In the 1930s he broke away from Hertzog's National Party to form his own 'Purified' National Party. The party fought the 1948 election on the issue of apartheid and defeated Smuts. Malan became the Prime Minister for introducing apartheid.

Mandela, Nelson (1918-   )

First became involved with politics during the Second World War as a member of the ANC Youth Wing. He was responsible for changing the ANC into a campaigning organisation. After the Sharpeville Massacre in 1960 Mandela questioned whether it was possible to continue with non-violent protests. He was one of the leaders of Umkhonto-We-Sizwe and was arrested in 1963. After the arrest of the Rivonia defendants he was accused of high treason and imprisoned for life. He remains in prison to this day and is recognised as the leader of black South Africa by many Africans.

Migrant Workers

South African industry depends on black labour. Workers may travel in from their Homeland. This can sometimes mean a daily journey of several hours. Other workers may live in compounds close to the coal or gold mines and return to their Homelands once or twice a year. Many workers also come from South Africa's neighbouring states.

Mixed Marriages Act Morality Laws

These were some of the earliest apartheid laws to be passed. They made it a crime for people from different racial groups to marry or have sexual relations. These laws have been scrapped as part of the reforms introduced by P. W. Botha.

MNR

The Mozambique National Resistance, also known as RENAMO. After Mozambique won its independence in 1975 white Portuguese army officers, supported by the white régime in Rhodesia, created the MNR. Their aim was to cause as much havoc inside Mozambique as possible. The MNR has no support inside Mozambique. After the election of a black majority government in Rhodesia the South African government took over the role of supporting the MNR.

Namibia

Until 1918 this was the German colony of South West Africa. The League of Nations gave the area to South Africa in 1919 as a Mandated Territory. South Africa was meant to look after the welfare of the people and prepare it for eventual independence. The United Nations directed South Africa to grant Namibia its independence and she is still illegally occupying the area.

Natal

The second British province of South Africa, which lies on the eastern seaboard.

National Party

The National Party is the ruling party of South Africa. It has won every election since 1948 and draws its support mainly from the Afrikaners.

National Convention

In the unrest following the Sharpeville Massacre the ANC called for a meeting of all groups to work out a peaceful solution to South Arica's problems. The government ignored the demands and there was a call for a national stay-at-home. It was after the failure of the National Convention that the ANC abandoned its long-held policy of non-violent protest.

Natives Land Acts 1913, 1936

The Land Acts set up 'Native Reserves'. These were the only areas in South Africa where Africans could legally own land. The Land Acts gave the Africans who constituted 80 per cent of the population 10 per cent of the land. The areas set aside under the Lands Acts were generally the poorest parts of the country and later formed the areas which became the Homelands.

Nguni

The Nguni are a sub-division of the Bantu-speaking people of South Africa. The Nguni-speaking peoples occupied the eastern part of the country. The two largest Nguni tribes were the Zulu and the Xhosa.

Orange Free State

With the Transvaal the Free State was one of the Boer Republics which fought against Britain during the Anglo-Boer War. Since 1910 the Orange Free State has been one of the four provinces of South Africa.

Ossewa Brandwag

The Ox-Wagon Brigade. This organisation was founded at the time of the centenary celebrations of the Great Trek. The OB saw themselves as the storm-troopers of the Afrikaner people. Their uniforms and organisation owed a great deal to Hitler's Storm-Troopers the SA in Nazi Germany. During the Second World War members of the OB were involved in acts of sabotage and several leaders were imprisoned, including J. B. Vorster, who later became Prime Minister.

Pan African Congress

The PAC split with the ANC in the late 1950s over the issue of Africanism. The ANC followed a policy where they believed that all the people of South Africa should have equality. The PAC believed in Africa for the Africans. It was the PAC who called for the Pass Law Demonstrations which led to the Sharpeville Massacre in 1960. Along with the ANC the PAC became a banned organisation and its leader Robert Sobukwe was imprisoned.

Pass Laws

The Pass Laws have a long history in South Africa. Since

the 18th century Africans living in white areas have had to carry some form of identity. Since 1948 the Pass Laws have been used as a form of control to prevent Africans moving to urban areas. Until the laws were abolished in the recent reforms it was a criminal offence for an African to be without his or her pass.

People's Congress
The Congress was held at Kliptown in 1955. Delegates from all races and from all over South Africa met to decide the South Africa they wanted. The result was the Freedom Charter. Security Police raided the Congress and documents confiscated were used in the Treason Trial the following year.

Poor Whites
During the inter-war years many Afrikaners were forced off the land by drought and low prices. They went to the towns but were unable to find work. They lived in squalor and poverty. Nationalist politicians were determined that white Afrikaners should not live in the same conditions as native Africans. The success of Nationalist politicians was winning over the poor whites to their cause.

Population Registration Act 1950
This was another foundation stone of apartheid and was one of the first Acts passed by the new government. The law classified the entire population according to a person's racial group. The Act recognised four groups: European, Asian, Coloured and 'Native'. Racial classification decided where a person could live under the Group Areas Act. There were numerous anomalies: brothers and sisters placed in different racial groups, visiting diplomats given 'honorary white status'.

POQO
After the Pan African Congress was declared illegal members of the PAC formed a secret underground army. POQO was responsible for attacks on white policemen and Africans who were thought to be collaborators. Umkhonto-we-Sizwe, the military wing of the ANC, by contrast tried to ensure that its violent attacks damaged property rather than people.

Progressive Federal Party
The PFP has been described as the conscience of white liberal South Africa. Until the elections of May 1987 the PFP was the main opposition party in the South African parliament. The PFP draws its support mostly from English-speaking South Africans in the Cape and also from 'English' suburbs of Johannesburg. Helen Suzman is the best known of the PFP members. She is a constant critic of the government.

Rivonia
Rivonia is a suburb of Johannesburg. Leaders of the ANC were hiding out in a farmhouse in Rivonia when the Security Police arrested them in 1964. Documents found at the farmhouse linked the ANC and Nelson Mandela, who was already in prison, with Umkhonto. Those arrested were charged with treason and put on trial.

Robben Island
A small island in Table Bay which houses South Africa's top security prison. Nelson Mandela and the other ANC leaders were imprisoned on Robben Island until they were moved to Pollsmor on the mainland.

SADCC
The South African Development Co-ordination Conference. SADCC was formed in 1980 shortly after black majority rule was established in Zimbabwe. The members of SADCC are South Africa's neighbours. Their aim is to develop the economies of the region so that they are less reliant on South Africa.

Smuts, Jan (1870-1950)
A Cape Town lawyer who moved to the Transvaal in the 1890s. After the Jameson Raid his sympathies were with the Boers. During the war he became an important Boer commander. After the war he rapidly became one of the most important politicians in the new Union of South Africa. He supported Britain in the First World War and became a member of the War Cabinet in 1917. Prime Minister from 1920-24 but was unpopular with Afrikaner Nationalists. Led United Party with Hertzog in the 1930s but the party split at the outbreak of War in 1939 when Smuts supported Britain again. During the Second World War he became much more widely known outside South Africa.

Soweto
An African Township outside Johannesburg. The name simply means South Western Township. It is a vast sprawling suburb covering 85 sq km and is home to over 1 million Africans who are forced to live there under the Group Areas Act.

Strijdom, J. G. (1893-1958)
Prime Minister between 1954 and 1958. Like many Nationalist politicians he was a hardliner from the Transvaal. Under his leadership the apartheid laws became much harsher. He himself believed that apartheid was a matter of the whites dominating the blacks.

Tambo, Oliver (1917-   )
Present-day President of the ANC, he joined the Youth League with Nelson Mandela in the 1940s and was a partner in the same law firm as Mandela. He was a defendant at the 1956 Treason Trial. After the banning of the ANC in 1960 Oliver Tambo left South Africa. He continues to direct the ANC from exile in Lusaka, the capital of Zambia.

Tomlinson Commission
A board of inquiry, led by Professor Tomlinson, was set up to investigate the possibility of setting up semi-independent Homelands. The government only put into effect the findings with which it agreed.

Transkei
The first of the Homelands to be granted independence. The Transkei is one of the tribal homes of the Xhosa.

Transvaal
The Transvaal was one of the two Boer republics which fought against Britain. It is the richest of South Africa's four provinces. The area around Johannesburg, known as the Rand, contains South Africa's gold and coal mines.

Tutu, Desmond (1931-   )

Leading Black South African church leader. In 1972 he was a member of the World Council of Churches and became Dean of Johannesburg in 1975. In 1978 he was made General Secretary of the South African Council of Churches and later became the first black Bishop of Johannesburg. He is well known for his opposition to apartheid and as a champion of non-violence. He has criticised both black and white in South Africa for their use of violence. In 1984 he was awarded the Nobel Peace Prize. Today he is Archbishop of Capetown the leading Anglich churchman in South Africa. Because he is known all over the world the South African government find it very difficult to silence him.

Uitlanders

The name given to gold miners who came to the Transvaal in the 1880s. Their way of life was alien to the Afrikaners and they were denied voting rights. The treatment of the Uitlanders was used by the British to justify the Anglo-Boer War.

Umkhonto-We-Sizwe

The Spear of the Nation. This was the group set up by Nelson Mandela and other ANC leaders after the Sharpeville Massacre. Umkhonto units attacked economic targets in South Africa in a campaign of sabotage. They claim that they have always tried to avoid casualties. This policy has now changed and Umkhonto make direct attacks on military and police targets.

United Democratic Front

The UDF was formed to campaign against the elections for the Coloured and Indian Parliament in 1984. The UDF is a coalition of all groups opposed to apartheid. It is the widest ranging protest group to have emerged for many years. The most prominent leader is the Revd. Allan Boesak. The UDF has been the subject of government pressure since its founding. Several leading members have been arrested on charges of treason, others have been banned. In February 1988 the government banned the UDF.

Verwoerd, Hendrick F. (1903-1966)

Editor of the right wing Transvaaler newspaper, he had links with Nazi Germany during the 1930s. He became leader of the National Party in the Transvaal in 1946 and was elected to Parliament in 1950. He soon rose to power and was made Minister for Native Affairs by Strijdom. Verwoerd was responsible for devising the idea of Homelands. After the death of Strijdom, Verwoerd became Prime Minister. He took South Africa out of the Commonwealth in 1961. In 1966 he was assassinated in Parliament.

Vorster, Johannes Balthazer (1915-1983)

A right winger from the Transvaal. He was a founder member of the Ossewa Brandwag and during the Second World War was imprisoned for his pro-Nazi views. He was elected to Parliament in 1955 and was a loyal supporter of Verwoerd. As Minister of Justice he was responsible for suppressing the unrest which followed the Sharpeville Massacre and for the arrest and imprisonment of Nelson Mandela and other black leaders. He was made Prime Minister after Verwoerd's assassination. He became President in 1978 but was forced to resign following a financial scandal.

Youth League

Part of the ANC. The Youth League became an important factor in the rise of the ANC in the 1940s. Prominent members of the Youth League were Nelson Mandela, Oliver Tambo and Walter Sisulu. The Youth League manifesto of 1944 outlined the programme and the tactics to achieve these aims. Some of the ideas were those of Africanism, though Nelson Mandela later rejected this in favour of a multi-racial South Africa.

Zulus

The Zulu were one of the largest tribes of South Africa. During the early 19th century the Zulu, under the leadership of Shaka, became the most powerful tribe in Southern Africa. Their influence and power continued until they were defeated by the British in the Zulu War of 1879.

Bibliography

Ruth First, *117 Days*, Penguin, 1965

M.K. Gandhi, *An Autobiography*, Penguin, 1982

Trevor Huddleston, *Naught For Your Comfort*, Fontana, 1957

Albert Luthuli, *Let My People Go*, Fontana, 1962

Nelson Mandela, *The Struggle Is My Life*, IDAF, 1986

Winnie Mandela, *Part of My Soul*, ed. Anne Benjamin, Penguin, 1985

Joyce Sikakane, *Window on Soweto*, IDAF, 1977

Mary Benson, *Nelson Mandela*, Penguin, 1986

Mary Benson, *South Africa, The Struggle for a Birthright*, IDAF, 1986

Brian Bunting, *The Rise of the South African Reich*, Penguin, 1964 Reprint IDAF Publications, 1986

Christopher Danzinger, *A History of Southern Africa*, OUP, 1983

David Harrison, *The White Tribe of Africa*, BBC Publications, 1981

Joseph Hanlon, *Mozambique: The Revolution Under Fire*, Zed Books, 1984

Joseph Hanlon, *Beggar Your Neighbours*, Catholic Institute For International Relations, 1986

Joseph Hanlon, *Apartheid's Second Front – South Africa's War Against its Neighbours*, Penguin special, 1986

Joseph Hanlon and Roger Omond, *The Sanctions Handbook*, Penguin Special, 1987

Alex Hepple, *Verwoerd*, Penguin, 1967

R. Johnson, *How Long Will South Africa Survive?* Macmillan, 1977

Govan Mbeki, *South Africa – The Peasants' Revolt*, IDAF, 1984

Mission to South Africa: *The Commonwealth Report*, the Findings of the Commonwealth Eminent Persons Group on southern Africa, Penguin, 1986

Roger Omond, *The Apartheid Handbook*, 1986

G. Parker & P. Pfukani, *History of Southern Africa*, Bell & Hyman, 1975

Leslie Rubin, *Apartheid in Practice*, Office of Public Information, United Nations, 1976

Keith Sorrenson, *Separate and Unequal*, Heinemann, 1976

Freda Troup, *South Africa: An Historical Introduction*, Penguin, 1975

Monica Wilson and Leonard Thompson, *The Oxford History of South Africa*, Vols 1 and 2, Oxford University Press, 1969

Donald Woods, *Biko*, Penguin, 1979

Donald Woods, *Apartheid: A Graphic Guide*, Camden Press, 1986

Reprints from *South African Yearbook, 1985*, Publications Division, South African Department of Foreign Affairs

Bureau of Information, *Talking With the ANC*, South African Government Publication, 1986

Southern African Facts Sheets, Southern Africa Editorial Services, Sandton, South Africa

South African Newsletters, South Africa House, London

New Internationalist, New Internationalist Publications, Oxford, May 1986

ANC News Briefings, Vols 9 and 10, published by ANC, Penton Street, London, 1985 and 1986